Trends in

Protestant Social Idealism

TRENDS IN PROTESTANT SOCIAL IDEALISM

J. NEAL HUGHLEY

KING'S CROWN PRESS
MORNINGSIDE HEIGHTS, NEW YORK
1948

TO

J. NEAL MAYNARD

*Whose generation is born
in groaning and travail,
but not without hope,
I trust.*

Preface

IT IS necessary that the nature and limitation of this work be kept in mind. In the first place the material treats only of American Protestant thought today, and of certain samples of that thought. There is no assumption that these are the *only* intellectual patterns, for there may be numerous others perhaps of equal significance. Moreover, although these selected representatives of contemporary Protestantism possess something of the character of symbols or types, there is nonetheless a certain individuality about each thinker which must not be obscured in the quest for significant classification. Perhaps it is best to regard their ideas as examples of *trends* or *emphases*.

Secondly, we concern ourselves neither with European thought on the one hand nor with American Jewish and Catholic literature on the other. Nor is there any attempt to survey the general history of Protestant social thought in the United States except that the first chapter provides some valuable historical perspective. What we seek is a description and an analysis of the most recent development in social philosophy emanating from certain theological sources in America.

It can be seen further that reactions to and views about all the specific social problems and institutions are not taken into consideration in our treatment. For instance, no picture is presented of a writer's ideas on race relations, education, family life, labor organization, the relation of church to state, the missionary enterprise, sports and amusements, social security, war and peace, and the like. Wherever specific opinions or attitudes appear in regard to such matters such opinions and attitudes are studied only as illustrations of the thinker's total and basic philosophy. For the ideas we endeavor to delineate are the fundamental conceptions about human nature, social change, social goals and strategies, political and economic institutions, and the relation of religion to these perennial questions.

A pivotal idea from which we set out is the study of each man in the light of his relation to the so-called social gospel. From this standpoint the whole book may be viewed as a commentary on the present state of the social gospel movement. The first and last chapters really constitute a unity in themselves whether taken singly or together, Chapter I being a historical orientation on the social gospel, with Chapter VIII coming as a description of the contemporary attack upon it. The pages in between offer detailed illustrations of outstanding and influential Protestant writers who are spokesmen for or critics of the social gospel viewpoint.

Observe again that attention is confined to social thought, no concern being taken of theological, ecclesiastical or general philosophical speculations save as these bear directly upon social attitudes and theories. The consequence is that many important literary products of the authors studied are treated slightly or ignored altogether. In some instances, as with E. Stanley Jones and Kirby Page, the strictly religious or devotional literature seems to be the most popular. But we are interested here primarily in works which throw light on the general problems of civilization, on political and economic ideologies, on theories pertaining to social goals and processes. Worship, church doctrine and speculative theology are of minor importance for our purpose. That is why, moreover, a large portion of the Neo-orthodox literature is of little or no value within the context of the matters under discussion in these pages.

Finally, this is an essay in criticism. The subjective element looms large everywhere, and the author is aware of the fact that he walks incessantly in dangerous territory. Many debatable evaluations are made, which fact when added to a certain sympathy for the aspirations of labor and socialism creates the suspicion that the writer is engaged in a piece of special pleading. It is true that the cause of Christian Socialism lies close to the heart of this expositor, and no attempt is made to disguise the fact in these argumentations. All we can say is that an honest endeavor has been made to wrestle with the details of the works under analysis, and special effort has been exerted to portray a given author's essential position with fidelity—though often with our own criticism added to the description. An important technique employed is to let the man speak for himself; and this in part accounts for the large element of direct quotation found in every chapter.

The author is much indebted for advice and practical aid to persons too numerous to mention by name. Special acknowledgment must be made, however, of invaluable criticisms and suggestions from Professors Schneider and Friess of the Department of Philosophy of Columbia University and from Professors Niebuhr and Bennett of the Union Theological Seminary, New York. During the period of intensive research innumerable acts of assistance were given also by my Canadian friends, the Reverend and Mrs. William E. Hordern of Union Seminary. Not least important was the help which came from my wife without whose efforts the preparation of the typescript would have been quite difficult.

J. NEAL HUGHLEY

Durham, North Carolina
January, 1948

Acknowledgments

THE AUTHOR is indebted to the following publishers and authors for permission to quote copyrighted material from their publications: The Association Press (Kean, *Christianity and the Cultural Crisis*); The Macmillan Company (Ward, *Our Economic Morality and the Ethic of Jesus, Which Way Religion?*); The Abingdon-Cokesbury Press (Johnson, *Church and Society;* Jones, *Christ's Alternative to Communism, The Choice Before Us, Is the Kingdom of God Realism?* and *The Christ of the American Road;* McConnell, *Public Opinion and Theology* and *Christianity and Coercion;* Ellwood, *Man's Social Destiny* and *The World's Need of Christ*); Harper and Brothers (Johnson, *The Social Gospel Re-Examined*); Rinehart and Company (Page, *Individualism and Socialism*); Charles Scribners Sons (Ward, *In Place of Profit;* Niebuhr, *Moral Man and Immoral Society, Reflections on the End of an Era, The Nature and Destiny of Man* (2 vols.) and *The Children of Light and the Children of Darkness;* Van Dusen (Ed.), *The Christian Answer*); The Oxford University Press (Visser 't Hooft, *The Background of the Social Gospel in America*); The Friendship Press (McConnell, *Human Needs and World Christianity* and *Christian Materialism*); Prentice-Hall, Inc. (Ellwood, *A History of Social Philosophy*); The Woman's Press (Ward, *The Opportunity for Religion*); The Board of Missions and Church Extension of the Methodist Church (New York) (McConnell, *The Church After the War*); Kirby Page, *Living Creatively, The Will of God for These Days, The Light is Still Shining in the Darkness, Now is*

[xi]

the Time to Prevent a Third World War, Capitalism and Its Rivals (pamphlet) and Property (pamphlet); Harry F. Ward (The New Social Order and Democracy and Social Change); Francis J. Mc-Connell (Democratic Christianity, Humanism and Christianity). The author is further indebted to the editors of the following periodicals for permission to quote material which is fully listed in the bibliography and notes: The Christian Century; Christianity and Society (formerly Radical Religion); Christianity and Crisis.

Contents

1

The Heritage of
the Social Gospel

1. *The Era of the Social Gospel*

IN REGARD to Christian phraseology perhaps no term has been employed in American ecclesiastical circles more frequently in the last half century than social gospel. It is not a little surprising therefore when, in seeking to understand the phrase in its various connotations or in its full historical setting, one discovers it to possess a quality of haziness and ambiguity. One historian of the so-called social gospel movement, who is very anxious to show that it is not limited to social action programs of churches in the early twentieth century, contends against the "false assumption that the Social Gospel first arose shortly after the turn of the century, with the work of the denominational social-service commissions." [1] Another such historian remarks that mid-nineteenth-century leaders who called their position "Christian Socialism" meant by this phrase "essentially a social gospel." [2] In the meantime, though books and articles are still being written about the social responsibilities of the church, there are misgivings on the part of those who would use the inherited terminology.

Professor F. Ernest Johnson confesses: "The term 'social gospel' is retained advisedly, though with full appreciation of the freight of misunderstanding that it carries. Until what it has stood for has been fairly appraised I do not care to have its standard hauled down." [3] In an earlier book he gives an explanation of the term which probably

[1]

would make it acceptable even to the most unqualifiedly neo-orthodox American theologian: "The social gospel is then an adaptation to the necessity, unrecognized by early Christianity, to live in the world. The church must either surrender in the face of a secularist order which makes a mockery of its ideals or set about changing that order." [4] Professor John C. Bennett, however, appears at times to be on the side of those who would let the term "social gospel" die a natural and perhaps an unnoticed death while retaining values which it has contributed to Christianity. He pleads for "Christian social action," noting that the more historic phrase "represents a particular combination of ideas that is in some respects dated." [5] Elsewhere Bennett remarks: "Sometimes our theologians indulge in polemics against the 'Social Gospel.' They make the mistake of not distinguishing between the fresh sense of responsibility for social institutions which came to us in American Protestantism in the form of the Social Gospel and the theological assumptions which have often been the frame for the Social Gospel." [6]

Partly because of the ambiguity of such language, and partly because of a continuing confusion over Christian social objectives and strategies, the era of the social gospel cannot be too categorically delimited. Observe that the implication contained in the very phrase "era of the social gospel" is itself a type of judgment suggesting that here is a period which has a beginning and an ending. The contention here is that despite its continued use the term has become associated with a certain climate of opinion—a theological liberalism combined with a pronounced social idealism and utopianism—which prevailed in the Christian world in the United States at a particular time. Our employment of the phrase carries the assumption that it is bound up intimately with such an era.

Before the middle of the nineteenth century American Christianity almost everywhere was church-centered and Bible-centered. Salvation was thought of in supernatural terms, being regarded as the possession of individual Christians whose "souls" were caught temporarily in this earthly prison-house. The "world" was the enemy of the Christian pilgrim, the divine message being predominantly one urging aloofness and judgment upon the daily concerns of mundane society. Aside from charitable activities as expressions of Christian love there were occasional piecemeal efforts at social reform designed to rescue men from the evils of an environment which hindered acceptance of the Biblical truths. Thus up to the middle of the nineteenth century American social Christianity was primarily a continuation and an application of the Puritan tradition, that is, in the broad sense of "Puritan." Popular religious movements like those of the Baptists and Methodists, for example, were basically anti-worldly and individualistic in temper and orientation.

In the seventy years between 1850 and 1920 a vast change came over the thinking of the most influential Christian leaders. On the one hand there was increasing application of science and historical criticism to theological ideas, while on the other an insistent demand for the application of religious principles to social questions. The time-span corresponds roughly to what we today call in theological terms the era of liberal Christianity, but in terms of Christian social ethics the era of the social gospel. The period of the so-called social gospel may be said, therefore, to fall mainly between the publication of Stephen Colwell's *New Themes for the Protestant Clergy* in 1851 and the death of Walter Rauschenbusch in 1918.

If the term were employed in a very broad sense as meaning the application of religious idealism to social institutions and problems, we could say legitimately that the period of the social gospel extends right down to the 1940's.* Dr. Charles C. Morrison in referring to the ideas of Archbishop William Temple declared editorially that "orthodox Christianity also has its social gospel." But by social gospel he means that the church recognizes "a unique responsibility for the character of civilization" while maintaining the purpose of "molding it in conformity with Christian principles." [7] Such a statement reminds us of the fact that this American social emphasis is but one expression of a widespread tendency appearing virtually throughout Western Christendom. Such a tendency, becoming ever more pronounced since the beginning of our century, has been in the direction of a more vigorous application of religious principles to

---

* Indeed, according to Professor McNeill in his *Christian Hope for World Society* (1937) the "social gospel" goes back to the institutionalized primitive church. But then he means by the phrase only a general Christian social "hope." With him the social gospel is found even in Augustine!

public questions. From this standpoint our country does not present us with a special, isolated phenomenon known as the "social gospel"; for in Anglicanism, Methodism in England, and even in Roman Catholicism a deeper concern for social reconstruction has been mounting for more than a generation.

Nevertheless, confusion appears partly because both the phrase and its associated ideas were cast within the context of a prevailing climate of theological opinion which is now under serious re-examination in the most progressive Christian circles. Such confusion is not likely to be cleared up soon because, in the first place, the theological rebels themselves sometimes defend the inherited language.* Moreover, not only is the framework of cherished ideals and hopes under profound challenge, but also there is amidst the disturbance as yet no clear-cut formulation of social goals and techniques. We are at present at the initial stage of an amazingly shocking demand for fundamental Christian reorientation, with energies being consumed largely in the clarification of theological principles. At the same time there seems to be little abatement in demands for social action—action reminiscent of social gospel imperatives—while religious thinkers continue to seek genuine and tenable grounds for such action. Meanwhile, because of this historic association of a certain kind of Christian social idealism with liberal theology, we shall take the phrase "era of the social gospel" to mean such a period as indicated above, namely, the time between 1850 and the conclusion of the first World War.

Hence in referring to the social gospel it is essential that the reader keep in mind the restricted sense in which we employ the language. In these pages it is inseparable from *social gospel idealism*. Our argument is that American social Christianity had an interesting and a relatively unique development in the period between 1850 and the First World War, the war itself providing the initial shock to this gospel-of-progress outlook. Although, as the succeeding chapters of

* Despite the fact that he calls the controversy over the present status of the social gospel "largely a verbal matter," Professor Bennett declares that to discard the phrase "might mean a loss of that vital sense of the social imperative that the Social Gospel means for everyone." *Christian Ethics and Social Policy*, (New York: Scribners, 1946), pp. 2 ff.

this volume disclose, there were numerous spokesmen for progressive social Christianity during the 1920's, the height of self-confidence and zeal seems to have been reached about the time of the War. The churches themselves entered the conflict as if it were nothing more or less than a holy crusade to make the world safe for democracy and religion. It is to *this specific era* in the United States—with its distinctively this-worldly outlook on political problems, with its fever for cultural progress, with its anti-theological bias and its faith in scientific method, with its pragmatic mentality in regard to the meaning of Christianity and its social task—that we give the name social gospel.[8]

2. *General Character of the Social Gospel Movement*

The movement which is summed up under the term social gospel was a many-sided one, being reflected in a variety of specific activities as well as in a number of fairly distinct forms. Moreover, it passed through several stages, although both as to forms and stages there was considerable overlapping. One possible reason for persistent misunderstanding in regard to this phenomenon is the tendency to look upon it in an over-simplified fashion as if the social gospel meant a specific, consistent expression of Christian idealism. Despite the fact that we are here dealing with a cultural era whose intellectual presuppositions possess many common characteristics we shall get only a distorted picture if we fail to see the increasing proliferation of the Christian movement, as well as its creation of sharply conflicting forms and patterns.

On this point the historical analyses have not helped us too much. Perhaps one of the greatest distortions, from the standpoint of historical origins and development, is found in Visser 't Hooft's *The Background of the Social Gospel in America* (1928). Many of the fundamental errors in the work are due to the deliberate ignoring of economic and political factors,[9] to the limitation of the expression of the movement to more or less churchly and theological circles, to an over-emphasis on the idea of an immanent God as if it were its whole theoretical basis, and to the assumption that the social gospel

[5]

arose only in the 20th century with such men as Rauschenbusch, Harry F. Ward, C. A. Ellwood and H. E. Fosdick. Visser 't Hooft is so exclusively concerned with the "theological" literature between 1912 and 1928 that he dismisses the pre-1900 era as of little or no consequence. Indeed, there is a tendency for him to make historical judgment on this era in the light of the evangelical tirades of Rauschenbusch, who naturally expressed impatience with what seemed to him the spiritual and moral inertia of the preceding generation. Our historian thus exclaims that "in the second half of the nineteenth century there was less participation [by American Christianity] in the public life of the nation than in earlier periods." [10] And his view on this point is made perfectly clear in the following statement: "England has had its social movement since the days of Maurice and Kingsley, who both died in the seventies. Germany had its period of strong emphasis on the social application of Christian principles led by Stoecker and Naumann between 1875 and the end of the century. French Protestantism was being awakened to social needs by men like Fallot before 1890. The Pope issued his famous Encyclical on the labor question in 1891. But America had little in the way of a social Christian movement before the beginning of the 20th century." [11]

Dombrowski's *Early Days of Christian Socialism in America* (1936) gives an excellent description of many aspects of the situation in the three closing decades of the last century; but the account implies that he is dealing with an era which is a prelude and an introduction to the real social gospel period. Aside from the fact that the story is cut short, it thus tends to throw out of proper perspective a period which was just as much a full, mature and significant expression of the social gospel as was the period between 1900 and 1920. From his treatment one could get the impression—though this is certainly not his own interpretation—that early "Christian Socialism" was not a complete, bona fide manifestation of the social gospel, an impression which Charles H. Hopkins deliberately intends to convey.

Hopkins' *The Rise of the Social Gospel in American Protestantism* is a thoroughgoing, extremely valuable catalogue of the facts. But the author takes the mass of details and artificially fits them into a quasi-organismic framework as if the social gospel was born

[6]

like an infant, grew to lusty youth and manhood and then received "maturity and recognition." He even goes so far as to separate the stages almost decade by decade: 1865–1880, 1880–1890, 1890–1900, 1900–1915. In an even more self-conscious fashion than Dombrowski he regards all the development up to the year 1900 as a kind of inchoate, inadequate striving which came to clearest and most perfect fulfillment in the work of the churches in the early twentieth century. His conclusion is that official endorsement "represented the full maturity of the movement and its most significant practical achievements. Such recognition heightened the prestige of social Christianity, opened to it the resources of denominational machinery, and provided new access to an immense audience." [12]

Now one does not wish to deny the fact that there have been developments, even tremendously important gains, in the application of Protestant ethics to public questions. There is something quite encouraging in the fact that a social emphasis made a pronounced impression on a considerable minority of the established churches, causing them to lose their exclusive preoccupation with irrelevant theological formulas and evangelistic appeals to individuals. But such acknowledgment is not identical with Hopkins' formula taking for granted a trickling stream of idealism in the mid-nineteenth century which flows to flood-tide in the opening decades of the twentieth. On the contrary, considering the decline of revolutionary Christian ideology characteristic of the closing decades of the nineteenth century, along with the growing bourgeois character of the ecclesiastical institutions in the years immediately preceding and following World War No. 1, one can build a plausible case for the cynical conclusion that the official acceptance of social gospel idealism, while certainly not an act of hypocrisy, was at least in some respects the degeneration of a magnificent hope.

It is instructive to note in the stretch of seventy years the variety of patterns through which the social gospel expressed itself. These may be summed up as vague protests (under which one includes preaching, evangelism, journalistic flurries, and protest meetings), utopian Christian social science, radical religious journalism, Utopian Brotherhood experiments, Kingdom of God movements, and social service activities.

[7]

The last decades of the nineteenth century are pictured by Dombrowski as the days of "Christian Socialism in America," the period from 1880 to 1900 witnessing a vigorous and courageous expression of social Christianity in American life. Aside from the stalwart figure of Walter Rauschenbusch in the twentieth century, these decades just preceding 1900 gave us virtually all the towering, militant champions of social gospel idealism—W. D. P. Bliss, George D. Herron, H. D. Lloyd, Henry George, and Edward Bellamy. Social institutions were not merely disturbed by the march of a defiant, unethical industrialism, the rise of numerous third parties, the rude awakening of an exploited labor, menacing outbursts like the panics of 1873 and 1893, the railway strike of 1877 and the Haymarket riot of 1886; but they were challenged by the radical, socialistic Christian Labor Union, the Society of Socialist Christians, the Brotherhood of the Cooperative Commonwealth, the Christian Commonwealth Colony, the Henry George Single-tax movement, Bellamy's Nationalist clubs, and the numerous books, pamphlets, periodicals and protest gatherings which spoke in no uncertain terms of the fundamentally anti-Christian basis of the American economic order.

Some progressive clergymen of this era accepted and utilized socialist theory even when they did not join radical parties. Leaders like W. D. P. Bliss, the Reverend J. O. S. Huntington and the Reverend W. L. Bull were members of an organization such as the Knights of Labor which was not unfriendly to socialist members. Although Hopkins brands the Christian Labor Union (1872–1878) as possessing a mere "religious humanitarianism," this movement was evidently a utopian socialism. The stirrings centered around the work of Henry George or of Edward Bellamy were so strongly anti-capitalist that they must be regarded as aspects of a utopian socialism. Those leading the Single-tax program or the Nationalist Club campaign knew that they were revolting against the whole framework of the laissez-faire economy, despite the fact that Karl Marx, as was natural, branded Georgism as American capitalism's last refuge.

We must remember that socialism itself was a vast, confused, many-sided type of thought to which not a few clergymen were hospitable even when they were not aware of the full implications of the ideas. The word itself certainly aroused no such hysterical fears as it often does today even in the most educated circles, notably in the business and journalistic world. Up to the 1890's it would seem that the word "anarchism" rather than "socialism" was the expression which automatically conveyed the idea of terrorism, lawlessness, and hostility to civilization and decency.

The era between 1900 and the gloriously "prosperous" twenties witnessed the almost complete triumph of capitalist thought in American culture, the outlawing even of the word "socialism" in religious circles, the failure of nerve on the part of a type of Christian social thought which in ideology spent itself in the repetition of an obscurantist Kingdom of God phraseology and in action contented itself for the most part with social service and innocuous humanitarianism. The powerful voice of Rauschenbusch wavered between a demand for a socialist society and an evangelistic appeal for a utopian Kingdom, while his excited hearers and supporters cheered his words, bought his books, and laid plans for the incorporation of his sentiments in ecclesiastical resolutions and social "creeds."

3. Varied Forms of Social Gospel Idealism

The first spokesmen for social Christianity in the nineteenth century were possessed of a strong ethical and religious indignation, but doubtless lacked a clear understanding of the revolutionary implications of their prophetic ideals. Their recommendations were inconsistent and self-cancelling; their reactions to socialism were confused, though often sympathetic; their preachments were spent in furious but platitudinous generalities and sentimental repetition of Biblical ideas. They possessed no tactics save those of evangelism, protest gatherings and publication of utopian literature. Such religion consequently, while calling attention to vast areas of human distress and social injustice, lacked both consistent social theories and effective techniques for implementation of exalted, far-flung hopes. When it did make gestures in the direction of a clear-cut conception of social processes and goals, it was tempted to cast such

[9]

thinking into the mold of nineteenth-century evolutionism, humanitarianism and perfectionism.

But in the last quarter of the century there appeared a remarkable number of preachers, editors, economists, sociologists, reformers, and leaders of affairs who perceived and expressed the need for a fundamentally different social order—a Christian Commonwealth, Cooperative Society, Brotherhood Kingdom, Kingdom of God, Mutualism, Social Democracy, Christian Communism. For a full picture of the many expressions of this rebellious, largely anti-capitalist religious idealism it would be necessary to examine the literature, politics, religion and social reform movements of the time. The social gospel historians, though their studies need supplementation in some ways, have done an immeasurable service in throwing a flood of light upon a religious situation which has hitherto been largely unknown or ill-conceived.

One of the earliest manifestations of the social gospel in this period was in the form of a utopian social science. Sometimes the emphasis was upon sociology or social research, at other times upon economics. An outstanding figure in this regard is Richard T. Ely (1854–   ), who has especial significance for both sociology and economics. Ely wrote numerous works many of which were used as texts by Christian study groups. He virtually identified the gospel with sociology, and recommended that theological students spend half of their time and energy on sociological materials.

A more unorthodox type of Christian social science was that of Henry George (1839–1897), author of the well-known classic, *Progress and Poverty*. George startled contemporary economists, statesmen and social theorists with the shocking idea that increase of wealth and technology led not to real progress but to increasing poverty and insecurity! He made some specific proposals, particularly the idea of the single tax, promoted a widespread social reform movement, and himself entered into active politics, running twice for mayor of New York City, in 1886 and in 1897. His Single-tax scheme, as well as his personal ventures into the political arena, was widely supported by the progressive clergy of the day.

Another movement religiously motivated and supported by many zealous Christian ministers and laymen was that which arose in connection with the views of Edward Bellamy (1850–1898). Bellamy's famous *Looking Backward,* which made its sensational appearance in 1888, declared that America was a society built on exploitation, competition and class privileges. It pictured the possible future society, the America (or rather the Boston) of 2000 A. D., as a social order in which such individualism and competition have been replaced by a freedom and an equality based on the nationalization of industrial production. Organized labor, both the A.F. of L. and the Knights of Labor, was friendly to the cause. Many ministers were active leaders, a considerable number looking upon Bellamy's "Nationalism" as the practical application of Christianity to society.*

Christian idealism in this period also revealed itself as a radical propagandist journalism. Such was the work of the Christian Labor Union, organized in Boston in 1872 and inspired not by Marxism or anarchism but by the utopian socialism of John Ruskin, Robert Owen and Fourier. The anti-capitalist motivation of the Union and its leaders was a pronounced feature. It published successively two radical papers, *Equity* (1874-1875) and *Labor-Balance,* the latter periodical giving endorsement in 1878 to the program and platform of the Socialist Labor Party and regarding the Party as an agency using political means to set up "communism." However, the whole program of the Christian Labor Union soon spent its force and the organization itself in six years came to an end.

Other instances of radical movements were the Society of Christian Socialists (founded in 1889) and the Brotherhood of the Kingdom, organized in 1892 at Philadelphia. The former, with the guidance of W. D. P. Bliss, charged capitalism with being fundamentally anti-Christian, while it looked upon socialism as Christian because it aimed at brotherhood. Its official organ was *The Dawn* which was published between 1889 and 1896. The latter movement, at first mainly a Baptist fellowship under the leadership of Walter

* While Bellamy's reform movement grew out of the work of a literary artist—*Looking Backward* is a romantic novel—the work of Henry George expresses two forms of social gospel idealism, both a utopian reformist program, including direct political action, and the development of a Christian economics or Christian social theory.

Rauschenbusch and Leighton Williams, was characterized by a vague utopian Kingdom of God idealism. Its influence in Christian circles, particularly in the form of annual conferences for the discussion of current social problems, was felt throughout the two decades preceding World War No. 1.

One of the most interesting episodes in nineteenth-century American church annals was the experiment in Christian communism known as Christian Commonwealth Colony. This was a community set up near Columbus, Georgia in 1896 under the inspiration of the ideas of Tolstoy, Bellamy and Henry George. It attracted some three or four hundred members and gained considerable sympathy and support even from such notables as Tolstoy, Luther Burbank, George D. Herron, Keir Hardie, and Jane Addams. Its organ, the *Social Gospel,* ran monthly for about two years. After an exciting start many serious internal problems soon developed, in addition to the fact that some compromises with the outside environment ultimately were necessary. Thus by 1900 the little fellowship had virtually disintegrated. It was a magnificent but disillusioning adventure upon an escapist enterprise designed to build a little Christian island in a world of greed, class division and industrial conflicts. Its failure was as dramatic and absolute as was its idealism.

Before calling attention to the special form of social gospel idealism which prevailed between 1900 and the First World War, let us beware of too great over-simplification by taking note of some important qualifying aspects of the period just described. In the first place it can be recognized quite easily that this whole impulse of radical criticism and Christian socialism was only a minority movement in religious circles. The masses of churches and the overwhelming majority of pastors were, as usual, characterized by inertia and devotion to the status quo, even in the realm of ideas. "Progressive," "liberal" or "social gospel" Christianity captured only the most creative and far-seeing minds of the age. Such rebellious idealism before 1900 was certainly not a universal, nor exactly a mass, movement; but from the standpoint of social thought it was the most distinctive and prophetic aspect of American Christianity. As such it gave form and definitive expression to that which was most significant in the on-going religious life of the times.

In the second place Christian Socialism did not die absolutely in the year 1900; for in 1903 there began a journal titled *The Christian Socialist*. In 1906 there appeared the Christian Socialist Fellowship which supported the Socialist Party of America, while making a plea on behalf of "International Socialism." The influence of this Fellowship was tremendous, such influence being created in part by the participation in the program of outstanding churchmen like Rauschenbusch,* Rabbi Wise, Charles Stelzle and W. D. P. Bliss. Many local branches of the organization were set up in the larger cities. It held a number of conventions, the largest taking place at Pittsburgh in 1910 when more than 375 delegates attended the session. In 1908 there was issued a manifesto proclaiming that socialism was desirable for creating an atmosphere and an economic environment suitable for the expansion of Christian ideals and sentiments. But the movement tended to decline after 1910, and rapidly disintegrated about the time of the war, though its influence was felt in certain small organizations even later. Concomitant with the rise and fall of this Christian Socialist Fellowship, however, was the official acceptance of the social gospel. It is this official, institutionalized social Christianity that dominates the progressive churches of the opening decades of our century.

In the third place, the social gospel was radical in the sense that it positively challenged the old order; but it was not possessed of revolutionary Marxist or Anarchistic conceptions, save in an isolated instance as when Lloyd embraced Marxism, or Herron accepted class conflict as inevitable, or when the Christian Labor Union toyed with the notion of "resistance to tyrants." Virtually all manifestations of this rebellious spirit were cast within the framework of positively religious principles or of a utopian socialism. There may be the temptation to dismiss hastily the whole phenomenon and to minimize it by virtue of the fact that these Christian Socialists did not fully understand the radical implications of their doctrines. But such a judgment would be rather premature. For as a matter of fact in a society where capitalism is entrenched there would have to be a long, intensive, sustained preparation for revolution. Even

* Rauschenbusch, however, was not formally a member of the Fellowship although he cooperated with it.

then, as Marx and Lenin themselves clearly recognized, no effort at revolution could have the remotest chance for success without the inner paralysis and breakdown of capitalism. Despite occasional depressions and many business abuses, no such threat to the economic system existed in the last half of the nineteenth century, which was indeed a period of pioneer, expansive, triumphant industrialism. It is enough for our tribute to the Christian fathers of yesterday that they felt poignantly the essentially anti-Christian nature of the capitalist ethos, and dared to protest fiercely against it even in the hour of its greatest victory.

The social gospel idealism between 1900 and 1920 became highly respectable, became in fact an established, formalized, creedalized, institutionalized program with all the gains and losses which such a process entailed. Since the general facts are now well documented, it will not be necessary for us here to endeavor to recount the details.[18] We may look merely at the nature of this phase of the social gospel against the background of the total movement, as well as against contemporary social forces in America. We may acknowledge in passing that there are considerable numbers who would subscribe to Hopkins' judgment that the "widespread acceptance of social Christianity throughout American Protestantism" betokens the "success" of the gospel in having reached many of its important objectives and in having gained "its most significant practical achievements." To many others, on the contrary, the results have been on the whole disillusioning against the background of a bourgeois culture whose surface in their judgment was merely being scratched while giant forces of maladjustment and disintegration marched on unchecked.*

During this early twentieth-century era which was dominated by humanitarianism, social service and social reform, expressed in more or less organized, official patterns, the Federal Council of

* In 1939, for example, Professor John C. Schroeder of the Yale Divinity School wrote: "Now after a decade one's confidence in this social gospel tends to be deflated. The multitude of reformist activities do not seem to have borne much fruit through these post-war years. . . . In short, all the good human efforts to make life more Christian or at least more decent seem like candles in a hurricane." *The Christian Century,* July 26, 1939, p. 923. His article bears the title, "A Deeper Social Gospel."

[14]

the Churches of Christ in America holds the central place. It is central because it is the most comprehensive, inclusive, and representative of all the Protestant bodies championing the social program. Its strength is felt increasingly on a national scale, both as a powerful church body in its own right and as the chief spokesman for the enlightened and influential denominations. Moreover, it contains most completely in its organization and program the two chief tendencies of modern American social Christianity—the impulse toward church unity and the impulse toward application of the gospel message to society. For about forty years (organized in 1908) it has been generally recognized as the authoritative proponent of the social gospel, as indeed a "sort of official keeper of the Social Gospel."[14] Yet it is truly a "federal" or federated council; for the constituent churches give only voluntary support to the program, whether financial or moral. Here we have not a genuinely nationalized, solidified, organic structure, but one allowing of almost complete local autonomy in regard to theological ideas, ecclesiastical polity, political theory and social action. Its inner strength and external influence are due largely to the relevance of its policies in giving expression to the increasingly felt needs of the progressive denominations, and to the enlightened, high-minded leadership enlisted in the execution of its program.

It is not our purpose here to recount even in outline the work of the Federal Council. As we have seen, there are numerous writings setting forth one or another aspect of the story, Hutchison's *We Are Not Divided* giving us a valuable comprehensive picture, as well as a bibliography of the principal pertinent sources. A much more risky, controversial thing must be undertaken, namely, that of trying to gain some significant perspective and judgment regarding the meaning and relevance of this program for the contemporary Christian task in America. One of the curious and yet understandable aspects of a situation experiencing rapid changes in the intellectual sphere is the desire on the part of many proponents of change to avoid offense to associates, especially to those with whom they have strong sentimental and institutional ties. Our religious situation is like this. Perhaps most of the American theological rebels seek to bring about thoroughgoing reorientation without institutional disturbances, indeed, without even interference with ecclesiastical loyalties save by strengthening them. Even more confusing is the not infrequent assumption that vigorous theological attacks upon liberalism, humanitarianism and social reformism will actually result in a more powerful and relevant social gospel, the case sometimes being described as an endeavor to revitalize the social gospel with a more profound theological content.

In the meantime misgivings still go on, perhaps in many cases without a clear consciousness of the basic issues. We must ask, therefore, what of the attitudes, loyalties, emphases and perspectives of those who still carry on this social gospel Christianity, and continue to speak of a "new social order" or a Kingdom of God? Is an overall shift in point of view necessary, or a shift in point of dominant emphasis? In the light of ultimate Christian social objectives, has social gospel idealism been moving in the right direction? Or must it acknowledge a fundamental illusion and blindness of perspective, with the result that a fresh approach to the social problem must be made?

4. *The Rising Wind of Neo-Protestantism*

Despite the glorious dreams of radical Christian idealism of the pre-1900 era and the many tangible accomplishments of the more recent social service emphasis, the social gospel faces a crisis not simply in the continued march of anti-spiritual political and economic forces, but through increasing demands for fundamental reorientation. A disturbing note was sounded when Dr. G. W. Richards in 1934, in an address before the Federal Council, declared that "there have always been unemployment and poverty, business depressions and panics, nationalism, wars and rumors of wars, domineering persons who ruthlessly exploit men for their own advantage." He charged that the content of the Christian message is not "conveyed by the popular and enticing phrase, 'The Jesus Way of Life.'" The gospel, he continues, is not "a device by which our capitalistic society is to be turned into an 'equalitarian brotherhood' in which men are made comfortable and happy without being made Godlike."

In the decade and more following this dramatic utterance we have seen new, unprecedented social disorders and equally unprecedented challenges pervading the theological world. The whole framework of Christian thought and of social gospel idealism is in fermentation.

What are the factors which are causing what seems to many a revolt against the social gospel? First, a deeper understanding has been gained in regard to many sobering and not in the least encouraging processes *within the church itself*. It can be seen, for instance, that despite all the revolutionary passion of the social gospel spokesmen, the American Protestant churches and their leaders have remained for the most part conservative in temper and outlook. Such churches and such men could promote only armchair revolution; for the moment the shadow of the class struggle appeared on the horizon, they were usually to be found specializing in counsels of caution, particularly to labor. Their ultimate reliance was upon a type of moral suasion, preaching and conciliation which overlooked the profound and tragic inequalities incorporated in American capitalist culture. Meanwhile the pews of the churches were filled increasingly with "successful" citizens whose Christianity was fully expressed in benevolence, goodwill and "social service." The theological rebels have perceived, therefore, the ironical fate of a social gospel professing to lead to the Kingdom but actually accommodating its policies to the restricted outlook of its money-minded supporters.

Other related factors within Christianity have contributed to widespread disillusionment. Ecclesiastical history, ancient, medieval or modern, has revealed the adaptation to the status quo of each progressive program of reform and of each change in the church's technique, with a concomitant loss of original vision or enthusiasm. Then too there was the temptation to subject Christian movements and institutions to the dominance of secular forces, parties and programs, with the not infrequent confusion of temporary social goals— often anti-religious in character—with the ultimate Christian hope. In this liberal humanitarian Christianity there was a loss of perspective or balance in regard to the relation of the individual to social change, there appearing a substitution for the romantic hope of individual conversion a new, not less romantic, hope of institutional re-

[17]

building. There was the failure to perceive the self-interest and pretension involved in even the loftiest programs, as we have seen, for instance, in the modern missionary enterprise in which Western churches have sought to dominate the so-called "younger" churches of the Orient. Add to all this the further fact that "progressive" religion has unconsciously distorted Christian doctrine and tradition, often disclosing a false interpretation or an arbitrary application of Biblical ideas. Jesus has been called an economist, a leader of proletarian revolution, or the founder of a democratic commonwealth. His ideas have been used by Christian scholars or leaders of affairs to defend capitalism, communism, techniques of social research and what not.

The world beyond ecclesiastical institutions has furnished its stimulus to intellectual revolution. A deepening awareness has come of the profoundly unspiritual, often positively unchristian, nature of the dominant institutions—the government, political parties, organized labor, business, even education. Not only has there been revealed a blatant, nihilistic paganism in Nazism, and a harsh, idealistic secularism in Sovietism, but in capitalism and democracy there has been a tendency to defy the highest Christian values, at times even to betray the gospel by making it serve as a chaplain blessing the politician's aspirations. Especially disheartening has been the manifestation of ruthless, irreligious, unethical elements in democratic or humanitarian idealism, such idealism not seldom being used as a cloak in which selfish interests have masqueraded as public welfare. Witness for example the now familiar device known as citizens' committees and citizens' fronts which exponents of monopoly capitalism even today sometimes organize to attack labor and to popularize their business objectives as if they were community goals. Socialism and the labor movement have added to the mood of disappointment. In addition to being a form of secularism, socialism has often been corrupted by its own leaders, some of them forsaking the cause when they actually held power and prestige in their hands. Moreover, it has been endlessly fragmented, most of the fragments adapting themselves to status quo conditions. Russia of course is seen as the supreme example of the potential fanaticism, secularism and opportunism of the collectivist enterprise. In both Europe and America, especially in the latter, labor has played opportunist, sacrificing its dreams of a new world and allying itself with power groups for short-range advantages. In international affairs, of course, power politics has continued largely undiminished, being revealed even in America's quest for power while she loudly and sentimentally denies the quest. As exhibits number one and two, the Protestant realists hold up the two world wars to show that we have experienced in a generation, despite all the Christian and democratic idealism, two global conflicts executed mainly by Christendom.*

Despite all the failure, disillusionment and criticism champions of religious idealism continue their preachments, while the churches and their agencies go forward in social action. Conferences are held continually, often ending in pronouncements and resolutions. Elaborate arguments are given in justification of the social gospel, like Professor J. T. McNeill's *Christian Hope for World Society* (1937) or Professor F. Ernest Johnson's *The Social Gospel Reexamined* (1940). A book such as E. Stanley Jones' *The Christ of the American Road* (1944), while it does not employ the phrase "social gospel," nevertheless contains most of the basic presuppositions and applications of social gospel idealism. The late Charles A. Ellwood, the sociologist, in his work, *The World's Need of Christ*, expresses the same traditional emphasis. The latter two volumes could have been written just as easily in the days of Walter Rauschenbusch, so far as the mode of thought is concerned. Occasionally thinkers who belong primarily to the new group of "dialectical" theologians make kindly gestures toward the "social gospel" or give careful expositions to suggest that the "essence" of its type of thought is being preserved. But no genuine reconciliation is probable in a day when the negative and rebellious spirit is at full tide.

American Protestant thought today, therefore, is largely divided into two great camps in so far as such thought relates itself to the

* A striking illustration of the kind of hard-headed realism characteristic of this rebellious school of religious thought is seen in Trueblood's *The Predicament of Modern Man*, 1944. While this book does not specifically set forth a *theological* position, it nonetheless mirrors in an arresting fashion the profound disillusionment with contemporary civilization pervading large sectors of the religious world.

[19]

social gospel tradition. There are in the first place men like E. Stanley Jones, Francis J. McConnell, Kirby Page, Harry F. Ward and many others who carry on in one fashion or another some phase or phases of this tradition. Whether they emphasize Christian socialism, Marxist principles, democracy, a Kingdom of God idealism, Christian social service, pacifism, or a rather negative ethical-religious criticism, they stand within the broad, many-sided stream of a gospel committed hopefully to social reconstruction. On the other side are the "realists" or neo-orthodox thinkers—including those professed liberals overwhelmingly influenced by the newer trends—who seek to refashion the whole structure of religious ideas associated with the social gospel. This latter group has taken a long swing in the direction of a neo-conservatism or neo-supernaturalism under the total impact of a profound disillusionment with all types of social reformism and all conceptions of cultural progress. Positively, they are seeking to rebuild Christianity as a faith which, while significantly relevant for the social problem, in their judgment comes forth again as a religion of eternal truth and reality free from the dangers of dulling its vision or weakening its force by any form of worldly entanglement.

2

Kingdom of God Idealism:
E. Stanley Jones

IN DESCRIBING the ideas of E. Stanley Jones, and even more in under-
taking to evaluate them, one is embarrassed by a peculiar dilemma.
On the one hand he finds it necessary to maintain a close connection
between *the man* and *his message*. In doing so he must recognize
that Dr. Jones is first and foremost an evangelist, indeed, in a very
real sense *only* an evangelist. *Time* magazine in 1938 referred to him
as the "world's greatest Christian missionary." This kind of tribute
can be well understood, for E. Stanley Jones is a tremendous preacher,
an indefatigable crusader, a leader of ardent, contagious religious
enthusiasm, and a man of enormous influence in Christian circles.
Moreover, there can be no doubt either of his profound moral earnestness or of his courageous application of the truth as he sees it to
the most delicate social issues. But here is the rub: while he writes
upon the most crucial political and economic questions of the day,
his approach remains exclusively in religious terms, in fact, in evangelical terms. Jones is not the scholar, the journalist, theologian, political leader, nor even the social reformer. Evangelism is his specialty,
and hence every political dissertation is fundamentally a sermon.
His economic doctrines are by-products of his missionary interests
in a literal and direct sense; they are mere applications of simple religious truths to society and its problems. There is thus the temptation to accept Jones' speculations as homilies or as elaborate extensions
of Sunday School lessons.

On the other hand there is scarcely any doubt that the evangelist is seriously offering *political* solutions. He endeavors to set forth a body of coherent social theory which is relevant to the task of institutional reconstruction. As a *body of social doctrine*, as a set of rational Christian social principles, we accept his speculations, and in so doing think we pay him some small tribute. We do not dismiss his arguments as mere "sermons," but weigh them earnestly as the views of a writer whose position represents a *certain type* of social thought emanating from religious circles. There is further justification for this as it appears that much popular Christian thinking on social issues is essentially that of Jones, who of course has the resources and experience sufficient to give such thinking a degree of expression, organization and plausibility.

Thus as a *body of social doctrine,* relatively independent of the question of personal earnestness or personal evangelical efficacy, we examine these ideas. We concern ourselves exclusively with the issue involved in the application of the Kingdom of God principle to economic, political, racial and ecclesiastical problems whose solution—or attempted solution—we as citizens in our time are called upon to seek. In the investigation of any body of theory proposed for application to complex human institutions and culture phenomena, intellectual honesty demands as great objectivity in analysis as it is possible for us to achieve. We must, so to speak, call an ace an ace and a spade a spade. It is inevitable, therefore, that we seek out, emphasize, underline both values and weaknesses in such doctrine, so far as our small resources permit. It will often be necessary to appear unappreciative by attacking ideas and illustrations which may have much value in a different context or with a different application.

The central aspect or emphasis of Jones' thought is the Kingdom of God, or "God's order." Certainly this is for him the one consuming idea, the primary religious doctrine, the supreme value or truth in the interpretation of life. He probably would not be satisfied with the designation of such a tremendous Reality as "idea," "doctrine," or "emphasis"; to him it is the objective, impending "Plan" or "Fact" confronting every man and every society, presenting to all and sundry the supreme challenge which they must accept—or reject at their doom. Throughout his ministry, in preaching or writing or conference, he underlines the Kingdom, making it central in both personal evangelism and social reconstruction. His books and articles are filled with interminable references to it, with expositions, defences, illustrations and applications of "God's order," the Kingdom.

There is "only one universal Order," he says. "Only one plan gathers up all the good of the lesser plans and eliminates their wrongs; only one plan is God's plan—the Kingdom of God." He promises that "if the Church will set Christianity in the framework of the Kingdom, it will probably be able to bring varying denominational emphases into a living blend." Speaking repeatedly of uniting the American denominations, he asserts that "once the Kingdom is discovered as central, then church federal union follows almost inevitably." [1] Again, "God must have a plan, and that plan is the Kingdom of God—God's order for human living." God redeems and rules in terms of Christ, and "the Kingdom is the Christ spirit regnant." When the Gospel of Luke refers to redemption, the Book of Revelation to salvation and power, the references are to that which is synonymous with the Kingdom. Jesus taught "redemption to the mind," preached "redemption to the soul," healed "redemption to the body." "To sum up: The Kingdom is redemption for the individual and for the whole of society." [2]

His earlier books are shot through and through with the same expressions, the same mode of reasoning. In *Christ's Alternative to Communism* he asks: [3] "In the next world crisis, for which we are definitely headed, will the leaders of thought and action see in Christianity the Christianity of the Kingdom of God on earth?" Elsewhere he agrees with Harnack's observation that Christianity, though having no "solutions," has "a goal and power to move on to that goal." That "most glorious goal ever offered to humanity," Jones adds, is the Kingdom of God on earth, "a Kingdom in which there would be no poverty, no classes, no sickness, and no sin, which would, in fact, be the Lord's year of Jubilee, a new world beginning." [4] In *The Choice Before Us* (1937) he titles four chapters as follows: The Kingdom, The Kingdom Personalized, The Kingdom Comes with Power, The Kingdom—the Key to Unity. [5] In this volume he essays to make a comparison of Nazism, Fascism, Communism and

Capitalism, making the bold charge that none is satisfactory and that only by immediate adoption of the divine "order" may we escape universal catastrophe.

Often his criticisms of Christian ideas, movements or programs are based upon the fact that the Kingdom is not made primary. He feels that in America, as we have seen, the root cause of denominational rivalry is the failure to emphasize this "Reality" above all. In the early history of the church, he argues, the fatal misstep was made by singling out Jesus (the "Person") and forsaking the "Order." By the time the creeds were written, so he reasons, the Kingdom had fallen into the background, or "was pushed into a heavenly world." Thus it was true of all the creeds, Apostles', Athanasian, and Nicene, that the "keynote" dropped out, the "order was gone," leaving a "crippled Christianity" with only a personal relation to a "Person-Saviour." [6] This same passion for the Kingdom led him to question the work and conclusions of the Madras Conference (1938), which Conference, he declared, discovered the church but left the Kingdom "on the doorstep." [7]

In line with the social gospel tradition the Kingdom of God is regarded as earthly, actually or potentially. In so far as it is a divine Perfection it is merely imminent, possible, surrounding our earthly structures like unexploded dynamite. It hangs over the affairs of men, personally and socially, as a tremendous, cataclysmic possibility.* But it is also a present reality in the world, boring from within, evolving, growing, expanding through all types of institutions or values, including the church. But most of all it is a reality and a possibility for *this present society,* for human history, within which domain it is destined to come to fulfillment. The mundane character of this "order" is described over and over from various angles. Will the spokesmen for religion in today's crisis, he queries, "see in Christianity the Christianity of the Kingdom of God on earth?" After discussing Christ's "alternative to Communism," he then offers

---

* "God's Order," he proclaims, "is standing at the door of the lower order ready to replace it. . . . It is God's Order over against man's system. This New Order breaks into the individual and the collective will wherever consent is given. It is the Final Way of Life offered to our expediences." *The Choice Before Us,* p. 23.

to believers the "next steps," namely the formation of groups and fellowships which will be "the Kingdom in miniature," Kingdom "cells."

Although the church will be very important, "the probable center of the Kingdom," nevertheless those outside organized Christianity may "turn out to be nearer the center than we"; for these marginal brothers too "are striving for the New Day, at least in some of its phases." [8] In a most arresting passage our evangelist avers: "We said that this Kingdom is built within the very foundation of the universe . . . it is also built within the very foundation of our own being. When the Kingdom comes we shall be truly natural; now we are trying to live unnaturally and are breaking ourselves in the process." [9] In another quite clear statement he contends that "God is determined to redeem history through History; and it [the Incarnation] has goal in that the Kingdom of God is to come on earth, so is to be the goal of all our longings and strivings." [10] The church is accused of having pushed the Kingdom "beyond the borders of this life," leaving out whole areas "unredeemed"—the economic, the political, the racial, the international.[11] Indeed, on more than one occasion Jones refers to the ideal order as a "communism," or an earthly "totalitarianism." The full meaning of Communism will be developed, he asserts in one passage, "in the Kingdom of God" which will be a "Communism based on love, good will, sharing, and a Common life." [12]

It would be a distortion of the truth, however, to charge Dr. Jones with making his basic religious "Fact" exclusively historical, mundane or natural. In numerous statements he lays emphasis on the transcendent, supernatural or unworldly aspect of the divine "order." He quotes Jesus: "My Kingdom is not of this world, else would my servants fight"; then goes on to say that the "New Kingdom" will break into the "process of nature and of history from above." "Its nature is different [from earthly orders]; therefore "the method and the weapons for establishing it are also different." It transcends Communism; for after the Communist society has been formed—that is, the inevitable "State Socialized Capitalism"—the Kingdom of God "will judge it and call for something better." [13] He calls the Kingdom process not merely "gradualistic," but "apocalyptic." He thus rejects

[25]

the theories which "have reduced the Kingdom to the coming of social reform," which in the spirit of "American activism" seek to "build the Kingdom" instead of endeavoring to "see," "enter," "proclaim," and "suffer for" it. Thus the revitalizing of religion in America "waits upon the rediscovery of the Kingdom of God content not as a gradualism or an apocalypticism but as both." [14]

It is perhaps unnecessary to pile up further quotations, for most of these thoughts about the Kingdom are reiterated over and over in all of E. Stanley Jones' major works which seek to apply his faith to the social task. His views of the Kingdom, of its nature, processes, demands and goals, as well as of its general relation to society on the one hand and to the church on the other, stand fully within the social gospel tradition. The fact that elements of transcendence appear in the conception does not remove it from this category, indeed gives greater justification for including it. Certainly Rauschenbusch was a champion of the social gospel; but his approach to the Kingdom as a natural ethical impulse working itself out in institutions and historical processes did not exclude the message that the Kingdom was divine and came down from above. Even so thoroughly socially-centered and psychologically-centered a conception as that of George A. Coe (for whom the Kingdom became the "democracy of God") was not wholly naturalized and humanized, as Professor H. Shelton Smith has recently reminded us.*

The distinctive element in Jones' idea of "God's Order" is that it is vitally and directly related to an earthly process as its goal, that it is fulfilled in history and in natural human institutions, with the result that social structures or processes are purged finally of selfishness, conflict, and other manifestations of sin. It is not just that this more or less humanized version of the Kingdom affects theological doctrine—in which we are not here interested primarily—but that the viewpoint is quite as crucial for social attitudes and policies,

---

* *Faith and Nurture* (New York: Scribner's, 1941), p. 38. Smith notes significantly that for Coe the Kingdom of God fellowship "includes both a divine and a human aspect," but that when he (Coe) "elaborates the meaning of the Kingdom it is usually the divine side that he leaves obscure or at least undeveloped." May we add that Coe at this point shows himself to be an almost perfect illustration of the conventional social gospel mentality.

for the evaluation of institutions, and for the formulation of political theory and method. Within this doctrine of the Kingdom there develops a characteristic though inchoate social philosophy, a typical approach to the solution of racial, political and economic issues. A further examination of Jones' ideas will reveal the validity of this contention.*

Before moving on to a consideration of social strategies and the problem of institutional reconstruction in general, let us look at the specific conceptions of Christ and of the church. To Jones, Christ is not merely the founder of Christianity, the author of faith and fellowship, the producer of the church and of Christian society, but he is co-equal with the Kingdom of God, in fact is its essence. "We, as Christians," he asserts, "have a starting point—Christ. To be a Christian is to respond to all the meanings you find in Christ." "We believe that in Jesus Christ we have an ultimate." There is "only one universal Man and only one universal Order." Indeed, "Christianity is Christ." [15] Christ is the embodiment of the Kingdom: "When he said that the Kingdom of Heaven is at hand, it was at hand in the very person of the Speaker and in the emerging society growing up around him." [16] Jones urges us to turn to Christ for the "meaning of the Kingdom," [17] for he is the "Kingdom personalized." In the same context he maintains that the "Supreme Order" and the "Supreme Person" are one, making our religion at once personal and social. Another utterance is that "the Kingdom and Christ are synonymous." Note that his book published in 1935 pleads not for Christianity's, but for "Christ's" alternative to the various politico-economic systems.†

*Other equally relevant data to prove how intimately the Kingdom is involved in history are as follows: it completes all the good found in earthly systems, it is a "plan" superior to, and to be substituted for, Communism and other "isms," and the laws of the Kingdom are "natural," built into the structure of daily social processes with an iron law of consequences for the observer or violator.

† The distinction between Christ and Christianity at this point is highly significant because Jones, like virtually all contemporary theologians, does not regard the totality of Christian culture or Christian civilization but only some idealized "essence" or theological principle (to him Christ the universal Man or God's Order) as "Christianity." Again, like religious writers of all schools,

There is of course no consistent or well-defined place which Christ holds in this essentially evangelical (rather than critical) approach. Sometimes the historic Jesus is made the be-all and the end-all of the Kingdom. At other times he is an originator or agent whose movement has fallen from grace since his earthly ministry. Many passages would almost imply that personal devotion to him in itself constitutes membership in the "Supreme Order," while other strong statements condemn a tendency to exalt him above, or at least apart from, the "Order." In at least one assertion [18] the writer seems to demand of believers the literal substitution of Christ the Leader for all earthly human leaders. In another passage [19] he boldly lifts Jesus to the highest conceivable pinnacle, as a cosmic Goodness above all men and as the norm for the idea of God: "You heighten your ideas of God when you think of him in terms of Christ," so that the highest compliment one can pay to a man or God is "to say he is Christlike."

The idea of the church—its nature, value, function, its relation to society and to the Christian movement—is likewise set forth in a vast assortment of utterances and expositions which cannot be reduced to a consistent pattern. There is a tendency at times to exalt the church as the supreme agent of Christianity, as the leavening force in society and as God's spearhead for the imminent Kingdom. While it is declared that God will not use to bring in his Kingdom any denomination "exclusively"—Protestant, Catholic, Oxford Group or other—"each of them holds within itself a phase of the Kingdom." Though the Kingdom is "larger than the organized Christian religion," "even as it [Christianity] is now organized, with all its faults," it contains "more of the Kingdom of God within it than any other system." [20] "The next great step in putting into operation the Kingdom of God is for each Christian church to conceive of itself as a part of that Kingdom, without exclusive rights and standing, and to recognize all other Christian bodies also as integral parts of the Kingdom." [21] Although no denomination "is synonymous with the Kingdom," "all denominations are more or

he violates this principle in defending the religious values in contemporary institutional life. Indeed, as we shall point out, he gets extremely sentimental in his idealization of democratic institutions as products of Christianity.

less approximations of the Kingdom." [22] The Church is "the agent of the coming of the redemption." It is patterned after the Kingdom.[23] Pleading for a nationally united American ecclesiastical system, the evangelist exclaims: "With all its faults the church is the best institution in American life," being the "greatest character-forming movement in our national life." "It has filled the earth with schools, hospitals, orphan and leper asylums, agricultural institutions—in fact with every type of institution for the purposes of human uplift." "The Church is the crusading body intent on creating a new divine society on earth." [24]

On the other hand one can find scarcely anywhere in current literature, sacred or secular, more fierce, terrible, shocking exposure of the weaknesses and failures of the church than in the writings of E. Stanley Jones. "The Kingdom of God," he warns, "judges the organized Christian religion just as it judges other systems, and again and again it stands condemned in the light of that judgment." [25] The denominations cannot spearhead God's New Order because God "is not going to bring it in by any messianic denomination," which incidentally is rejected exactly for the same reason that "any messianic race or class" is rejected.[26] The churches are racial churches; hence is "the brotherhood of Christ turned into a racialism! This is what we have reduced it to!" [27] Even Communism is "juster" than Christian capitalism and its puppet churches: "When the Western world was floundering in an unjust and competitive order, and the church was bound up with it and was part of that order, God reached out and put his hand on the Russian Communists to produce a juster order and to show a recumbent church what it has missed in its own Gospel." [28]

In *The Christ of the American Road*, after giving what he calls a "first judgment on the Christian movement" which is "favorable," he then releases devastating blasts.[29] Here are some utterances picked at random from this penetrating critique: The "Christianity of America differs fundamentally from the Christianity of Christ." "The Kingdom has been marginal; the church has been central. Hence the Church has not been the embodiment of the New Order; it has been an aggregation of worshiping individuals." "We have reduced this majestic coming of the Kingdom to progress in social justice amenities." Not possessed of the Kingdom, the "church sinks into petty irrelevancies and marginal issues; it does not confront the whole of the life with a total demand for a total obedience in the total life." "The distinction between those inside the church and those outside is breaking down. And mind you: if there is no outer difference between the Church and the world, there is no inner." "This commercialization has permeated the whole of American life—including, I am sorry to say, the Church. It has invaded the ministry; and a man's 'grade' is often determined, not by his sacrificial service, but by his salary." "No wonder the pulpit lacks moral authority in American life. It is too much like American life; it is not greatly different, so its message is not greatly different."

Recalling our previous contention that the Kingdom of God is pivotal in every aspect of Jones' thinking, the reader can observe in nearly all the quoted passages how this basic idea is utilized. Both the devotion to the church and the vigorous criticisms of it in part grow out of the meaning of the institution for God's coming absolute "Order." The early church of the immediate disciples *was* the Kingdom because it was the germ of the "Order" proclaimed by the Master. Although later generations corrupted this true church, this "reign of God" in the form of an early Christian communism, the spirit or concept of the true church remained buried within the decadent, worldly institutionalism of historic (even Catholic) Christianity. If we can revive the church, therefore, by stripping it of its ecclesiasticism and pagan cultural accretions, if we can check its concentration upon itself as an end-in-itself, if we can raise once more into central focus the passion for the ancient yet ever new Kingdom, then we can see that the church is after all the real agent of God. On the other hand since the church as presently constituted is not the Kingdom itself, it must face two major facts. First, in so far as it refuses to make the perfect Order primary, it has betrayed its genius and must be condemned by the judgment of God Himself. No relativism, not even the church, must set itself up in opposition to the imminent reign of the Divine. Secondly, in so far as non-ecclesiastical institutions allow themselves to be infused with the Divine Spirit, yield themselves to be instruments for revolutionary change, they too are agents of God along with the church—or perhaps even better than the church. Communism, for instance, though corrupted by methods of coercion, is prophetic of change, and indeed is God's own judgment upon the apostate church itself. Hence in Jones' writings we witness the phenomenon of a man who in one breath strongly condemns all ecclesiasticism, including that of a temporary Madras conference, and in the next becomes the militant champion of what would almost certainly be a super-ecclesiasticism—the total organization of all the churches of America and even of the world into a single federated system! [30]

In getting a comprehensive understanding of the view of Russia contained in these pages one must keep in mind certain over-all attitudes which govern Jones' approach. In the first place there seems to be no fear of Communism such as usually lies in the background of so much American social thought, religious and political. While Russia has made a profound impression on this sensitive spirit, reactions are controlled largely by a variety of factors some of which strongly attract, while others just as strongly repel. Hence it is probably better to designate Jones' position not so much as a *conception* of Marxism as a series of moods and shifting attitudes. At times Russia is taken as a challenge, at times as an example, at times as a threat, at times as a great inspiration. Hence she is both violently praised and violently condemned. In the light of the Soviet experiment Christianity is held up on the one hand as possessing an incomparably superior "plan" which is even "more scientific than Marxian Communism." [31] When compared with the Kingdom idea Russia at one place becomes a central agent in its coming, at other places a corrupt version of it or its dangerous foe.*

Utterances of praise are often unhesitating. Even Jesus would approve of much in Sovietism! It offers a "detailed," "decisive" program as an "alternative" to Christianity; and though it is "anti-Christian," "there is so much in Communism that Christ would approve." [32] He would endorse the attempt to create a "cooperative" society, the prison system "without revenge, without stigma," the school system which undergirds and supplements parental care,

* On the whole, however, our impression is that the attacks on Russia considerably outweigh the praises and challenges. Resentment toward undesirable elements in Marxism is expressed with great frequency.

the "attitudes toward different races" which make discrimination a criminal offense, and the "People's Courts" where justice is done without "legal quibbling questions." [33] Russia has taught us that the individual can be changed by the changing of the economic order." [34] Reflecting upon a visit to a Russian school he notes: "The child pronounced the system [Sovietism] all right. . . . Convictions laid in the mind of the child last . . . the only really lasting ones." But "Christian democracy will not last unless the child inwardly accepts it." [35] "Russia has the seeds of democracy within her." [36]

There are many vital resemblances between Communism and Christianity. The latter is in "direct opposition" to Fascism and Nazism, but has "much more in common with Communism," being "nearer in spirit to it." [37] Although Christianity will not be a Marxian Communism "shot through and through with force and compulsion and hate and intolerance," it *will be* a "Communism based on love, goodwill, sharing, and a Common Life." [38] Indeed, true Christianity will be "a holding of the means of production by all in behalf of all; a brotherhood that would make life a family instead of a feud; a sense of destiny and direction coming from the fact that God is in the corporate life." [39] Jesus laid down three basic communistic "principle-practices": (1) elimination of acquisitiveness, (2) support according to need, (3) contribution to society according to ability. These are the foundation stones upon which we shall build, or rocks upon which we shall stumble to our doom." [40]

Jones sometimes uses the word revolution or totalitarian as appropriate for the Kingdom, speaking frequently of Christian revolution or Christian totalitarianism. "The Christian revolution," he boasts, "stands for the rights of a man as a man apart from race and birth and class," while all other revolutions stop at class, or color, or race, or nation." [41] The New Order of Jesus "would be more totalitarian than the Totalitarianisms of the day; more communistic than Communism and more individualistic than Individualism." [42] There is no doubt that the evangelist clearly understands what he says, and he goes all the way to a revolutionary Christian communism: "I am persuaded that if Christianity were really applied again, [as it was at the beginning] it would result in some form of collective sharing closely akin to Communism. Closely akin, but minus Communism's class war, minus its ruthlessness and compulsions, minus its denial of liberty and materialistic atheism. I grant that there are a good many minuses there!" [43]

However, as noted above, there are many strictures on Communism or Marxism. It is condemned for violence, dictatorship, intolerance, economic determinism and irreligion. It is also charged at times with working only on the external and institutional. After smashing the old order the Communists, he claims, achieve only change "from the outside in and not from the inside out," trying to impose a new regime by force.* The Soviet spirit is wrong . . . trusting in "all human effort," possessed of a cynical humanism, while "endeavoring to put into effect the Christian program without the Christian power." Moreover, "when all is said and done," the Soviet system is a "Kingdom of the Mass Man," in which the individual is overwhelmed by "mass suggestion, mass propaganda, and mass action. Individual freedom is reduced to the vanishing point." [44] He finally rejects Russia in favor of Christianized Americanism: "Democracy is more interwoven with the texture of her (America's) life and more inherent in her faith than in that of Russia." Russia's "faith in man is based on a humanism and is not supported by a moral universe. Her faith in man therefore cannot last unless she gets a larger faith." †

Indeed, both *Christ's Alternative to Communism* (1935) and *The Choice Before Us* (1937) were written primarily to prove that Christianity is superior to Marxism and Fascism, both in spirit

* *Christ's Alternative to Communism*, pp. 154 f. But he turns right around and says the opposite: In looking at the Russia of 1934 you are "looking at an entirely different people" whose "whole life has been changed—its tempo, its temper, its spirit, and its goal. For good or ill they are a different people." (*Ibid.*, p. 161). He also says (*Ibid.*, p. 175) the Russians as their next step will "emphasize individual culture and development."

† *The Christ of the American Road*, pp. 106 ff. Note that this book was written in 1944 after Jones had returned to America and after a decade of rising American disillusionment with the Soviets, particularly after the apparently ruthless tactics employed by Russia in foreign relations. The former works which praise Russia so highly came forth in the decade of the depression when our economy was in the doldrums. Could it be that the political and economic situation has some effect upon the tone or outlook as between the earlier and later literature?

and purpose and in practical political policy.* For Christianity likewise has its socio-economic system, its "plan," its divine New Order which must replace these inadequate, ever-failing mundane systems. He warns: "Christianity has been preached to death. We must get hold of a program for world reconstruction and boldly apply it, lest again the Communists seize world power from the hesitating hand of Christendom." Which is to be the "Pole Star from which humanity will take its reckoning for its future course— Marxian Communism or the Kingdom of God on earth? Upon the answer to that question hangs the destiny of our race." [45] He outlines the broad principles of the Christian "plan." [46] "Blood and confusion and chaos can be averted. The Christian way is the way out." "The Kingdom of the Atheistic Mass Man and the Kingdom of God are at the door of the world. This generation may have to decide which one it will take." [47] We have already seen that when God's Order is given literal political embodiment it becomes in the evangelist's opinion a Christian Communism in which the family idea is applied to all human institutions and relationships.

Before going on to a glance at his general conception of man's nature it is well to note that his resentment toward the evil in capitalism is as great as it is toward the newer European "isms." Capitalism is failing, is inadequate for human needs. The world must come to the "conclusion that the present competitive order is impossible and is breaking down—we are fast approaching that point now." "Capitalism, it will be seen, while containing a demand for greater equality, brought over with its radicalism a wrong to man." [48] This decadence and coming doom can be seen in under-paid labor, the general failure of purchasing power, over-production, paralyzed capital, widespread and continuing unemployment, and giant depressions, all of which together brings on "this world-shaking upheaval

* It is not necessary to linger on his specific reactions to Fascism. He is unqualifiedly opposed to it, regards its doom as inevitable, its appearance as caused by desperation and a breakdown in liberty. At one place, of course (*The Choice Before Us*, p. 77), he explains it in typical over-simplified Marxist terms as capitalism's refuge. At any rate Christianity supplies all the values which it could possibly have (*Ibid.*, p. 96).

[34]

on the edge of which we now stand." He condemns the capitalist system as a whole, quoting approvingly a passage from Sherwood Eddy: "Our present economic order is founded on the profit motive, monopolistic ownership and consequent class inequality, injustice and strife." [49] If Jesus' saying, "Ye cannot serve God and mammon," were translated into modern terms it would read: "ye cannot serve God and the private-profit motive." [50] "The idea that a man would not work except for the profit motive is being disproved in Russia and around the world whenever it is tried. . . . A competitive order cannot provide a cause; a collective order would." [51] The present maldistribution of wealth is unchristian; so is the tendency to exalt "property rights" above "personal rights." Hence wealth must be redistributed.[52]

Christianity is not inherently bound up with capitalism—indeed must of necessity free itself from its deadening hand. "We have gone as far in spirituality as we can under the competitive system. We are blocked at every turn in further individual and collective spiritual development. Christianity under this order seems an absurdity and unworkable. It is just that—under this order." [53] "Christianity must, on no account, be considered bound up with capitalism and its destinies, for it was here long before capitalism arose, and it will be here long after it has been changed; or if it cannot be changed, then supplanted by a juster social order." [54] Furious assaults are likewise made in *The Choice Before Us*.[55] Also in *The Christ of the American Road* he accuses: "This order periodically jams up at the place of distribution. It has the motive for production, self-interest, but it hasn't the motive for distribution, other-interest. Hence our economy periodically overproduces; then there is unemployment and depression. These cycles have been recurring with increasing frequency unless war comes along and eats up the surplus produced." [56] But in this volume Jones has greatly reduced the fury of his criticism. He moves a long way in the direction of a compromising religious reformism, instead of continuing his strong advocacy of a revolutionary Christian communism. He is much more concerned here with applying to American life his "Principle of the New Man," that is, a harmonizing, synthesizing (Hegelian?) principle, seeing

[35]

some great good in everything, even in pragmatism, materialism, the American "frontier mind," nervous energy and "our love of success."

Let us begin at just this point to see what the basic outlook of the evangelist is on human nature, social institutions, political processes and strategies. In regard to human nature Jones is an idealist of the most extreme type, though he would no doubt prefer to call his view "realism." By "realism" he means of course what he regards as the Christian faith in the divine possibilities of man and society. Christ, he affirms, was a "stark realist." * The Gospel is "realism" because it is founded on the "very nature of God" and not on "an idea that God had," which would be "idealism." Such realism is both revolutionary and conservative since God is "on the side of the fermenting wine of revolution" and the side "of retaining wine-skins." Hence Jesus was "utterly realistic," and in this he was both religious and scientific.[57] Jesus has been called "the Son of Fact"; he is "grace manifested," the "uncovering of reality and is therefore sheer realism." "He did not paint a Utopia, far off and unrealizable," but a "Kingdom of Heaven within us" which can be "realized here and now." Any of the terms such as idealism, optimism, utopianism, romanticism would be applied unhesitatingly by most social theorists to such moods and attitudes as these. E. Stanley Jones is without doubt a perfect Christian romanticist in his view of man individually and collectively.

His confidence in the changeability of human nature is almost unbounded. "Put together the fact that it is human nature to change, and that it is divine nature to change human nature, and you have

---

* *Is the Kingdom of God Realism?*, p. 16. Observe the slippery juggling of the terms "realism" and "idealism." We note this same seizure of words for adaptation to his purpose in the use of "totalitarianism," "revolution," "communism," "individualism," even "pragmatism" (*The Christ of the American Road*, p. 246). He employs almost any idea, concept, or impulse by giving it a spiritualized meaning and Christian application. In short, Jones has no respect for traditional usages and meanings, even in philosophical literature. All his books are sophisticated sermons, and he will grasp any illustration, phrase or human trait which makes vivid the point uppermost at a given place in the argument. Hence almost nowhere is there any real consistency in his theories from the intellectual point of view.

the stage set for vast changes." "We can provide for humanity any social heredity we desire. It is all in our hands. Suppose we provide a new social heredity on a large scale, and suppose people respond to it on a large scale, then we could remake humanity in a short space of time." [58] Hence the optimism about prospects for radical social change. "If we can get men to respond to the emotion of the ideal of the Kingdom of God on earth, then vast changes could be made in the total life of humanity, and they could be made in one generation." [59] "The possibility of a world awakening taking place through the Lord's Year of Jubilee gives hope that Christianity" is not only capable of "personal conversion" but of a "workable program for world reconstruction." [60] "The foundations of the Christian way have been laid in the world mind—it is latent, awaiting the touch of Christian daring." [61] He remarks in the Foreword of his book, *Is the Kingdom of God Realism?*: "The comment of a very thoughtful layman interested me: 'Within ten years the viewpoint and attitude of this book will become common property in the Christian Church, and when it does, it will create a Christian revolution.'" [62]

The evangelist thus sees prophetic stirrings in all sorts of situations, in some places which are most outlandish. He pictures the Kingdom of God as now dethroning earthly princes, Christ becoming Lord in all the world, even in the Kremlin, Communists bringing in God's New Order, British politics and Rotarian business "sensing the inherent and final truth that no man should command who does not serve." [63] He thinks that class-centeredness may wither away in Russia; that "the more men become scientific the more they will become Christian"; that the European nations have "voted to disarm" and "are moving toward a co-operative society," led by Denmark.* And his temper did not alter fundamentally with the passage of the gloomy years between 1935 and 1944. In the latter year he published *The Christ of the American Road* with its incredibly sentimental glorification of American culture. While there are notes of doubt and pessimism here and there,[64] he boasts that American

* *Christ's Alternative to Communism*, pp. 227, 246 f., 278 f. Of course these lines were written before the second Global War, and today must surely not be read by the evangelist with too great relish.

[37]

democracy is largely the offspring of Christian faith, that Christ is the cement of our civilization, that we have the "raw materials" to produce an "American interpretation of the Kingdom of God." Though in an ultimate sense this faith may not be ruled out categorically as extravagant, it nevertheless leads Jones to idealize and sanctify many of our most egocentric American traits: materialism, "our love of success," nervous energy, mass production, our "frontier mind," our "love of variety," love of freedom, pragmatism, and faith in the future.[65]

Consequently he spends much effort in making strong appeals to individuals and groups to forsake their interests for the Christian way. At the conclusion of one book, *The Choice Before Us*, he makes a special, direct plea to all of the following groups, as broad cross-sections of the national population: to the youth group, to "the men of big business, or smaller business, the Industrialists," to labor "to go Christian," to the universities to get "behind God's order," to governmental authorities to put "the Kingdom of God down through governmental processes," to preachers to stop dealing with "burnt-out issues," and to "men and women of the pew" to join their pastors in the "Great Adventure" of being a Christian.[66] Elsewhere he exclaims: "Christians of America, unite! You have your greatest world opportunity for the reshaping of the world in doing so. You have nothing to lose except your dividing walls!" [67]

Thus Christianity in his judgment can not only turn the world upside down in an incredibly short time, but it can do so without letting loose the forces of violence, class hatred, and bloodshed. His faith in the capacity of human nature to undergo radical change adds to his confidence in the non-violent revolutionary possibilities of religion. Men are merely intellectually blind to the tremendous values in the Kingdom ideal; but they are beginning to awaken. If the light of truth is turned on a little more fully by evangelism, education, mass appeal, conferences and fellowship meetings we may be sure that the Lord's Year of Jubilee will arrive shortly upon the earth.

3

Christian Sociology:
Charles A. Ellwood

IT IS NOT LIKELY that one can find a better representation of the social gospel outlook than in the thinking of the late Charles A. Ellwood,* the well-known sociologist of Duke University. He exemplifies a remarkable passion for scientific and sociological studies combined with an earnest desire to apply the fruits of such studies to social problems. His academic interests extend over a wide territory covering sociology, social psychology, social philosophy and religion. Although a layman he has possessed almost evangelical zeal for religion, both for the investigation of the nature and value of religion and for its practical application to all manner of human problems.

Professor Ellwood thus was the champion of a strong social and religious idealism which seeks nothing less than the total reconstruction of modern society. A chapter in one of his most recent books expresses in its very title what was his over-all enduring concern through the years—"the Christian reconstruction of our civilization." [1] Dr. S. M. Cavert of the Federal Council of the Churches of Christ in America in the foreword of this volume remarks: "As *The Imitation of Christ* summoned men of the Middle Ages to a following of Christ in their personal living, so this volume would call

---

* Dr. Ellwood died as the final draft of this manuscript was being prepared. In 1944 he retired as a member of the Duke University faculty, and was seventy-three years old at the time of his death in September, 1946.

them to a modern imitation of Christ in the whole range of social and international relationships. Nothing less than this, it is vividly shown, can save civilization."

For the tremendous task of world transformation there must be, according to Ellwood, a complete marriage between religion and science, that is, between a practical Christian idealism and sociological theory and method. Or expressed otherwise, the principal need of modern men is the development of a Christian Sociology or Social Science, a task to which this scholar of Duke University has given himself with sustained devotion. But the job is not merely a theoretical one, not simply the elaboration of carefully constructed social principles and techniques. As he notes in an early work, "the problem of life presents much more than a problem of knowledge. It is even more a problem of motives and of will attitudes—of aspirations, desires and determinations. The human world is governed not alone or mainly by thought, but even more by emotion." [2] Hence the overwhelming importance of religious vision and consecration. "The religious spirit is the spirit of devotion to ideal social and personal ends and of the consecration of individual life to these ends." Science, therefore, must utilize religion as a "spring of social idealism" and religion must accept science for the responsibility of drawing "plans" and furnishing "means." [3]

It is not surprising to find in Ellwood's writings a strong indictment of the evils of modern life. Ours is a "semi-pagan civilization," a culture into which the inherited unspiritual Renaissance elements have resurged. "Modern civilization," he accuses, "has been troubled by the recrudesence of pagan ideals of life. Power and pleasure have remained its chief ideals." [4] " 'Paganism' or 'barbarism' evidently underlay, in the main, the culture of Greece and Rome," he continues. "It also evidently underlies the culture of the present, since it is that stage of culture which lies back of our civilization and from which we are but just emerging." [5] The Great War of 1914–18 revealed these menacing, unspiritual, pagan forces. [6] We can no longer remain "half pagan and half Christian"; for the world must become "speedily Christian" or "speedily pagan." [7] In fact "our age is an age of machines and of physical science, which temporarily, at least, have crowded into the background all spiritual values." [8] What

Americans worship most today are "physical strength, personal beauty, intellectual power, and financial success." [9] He quotes approvingly from an observation of John Dewey: "We seem to find everywhere a hardness, a tightness, a clamping down the lid, a regimentation and standardization, a devotion to efficiency and prosperity of a mechanical and quantitative sort." [10]

After the outbreak of World War No. 2 Ellwood acknowledged that our civilization is disintegrating. "Disorganization and conflict in human relations," he warns, "have been increasing for more than a generation, and are now world-wide." The thought of Jesus about human relations "has been increasingly ignored or set aside as impractical for nearly a generation." [11] In this book he accepts without question the sociological-philosophical critique of P. A. Sorokin who charges that ours is a "sensate" era which exalts the external, material aspect of culture and which has lost all genuine belief in the reality and validity of the spiritual. Ellwood thus brands our communities as being "body-minded" and "thing-minded," as possessed only of a vision "absorbed wholly in the things of this world." [12] He further declares: "But there must be a reason for the selfish competition which has set nation against nation, and class against class, to say nothing of conflict between individuals. The reason, according to Sorokin's interpretation, is that men, like the brutes, have tried to live by the sense satisfaction." [13] Referring to the Harvard sociologist's outstanding treatise in four volumes, *Social and Cultural Dynamics* (1937–41), Ellwood concludes that "here at length is a scientific diagnosis of our civilization which casts a flood of light on all its troubles. A spiritual religion, such as Christ taught, and a sensate civilization are, as we have tried to show, two incompatibles." [14]

His indictment ranges over the whole of our institutional framework. The economic order is pagan and unchristian, industry being still "dominated by purely materialistic interests," while the property system, at least in capitalist society, is but a "modification of the primitive hunting pattern." [15] As for international affairs, "the Christian should be shocked that the world continues to be governed by the method of murder and the threat of murder." [16] The state is basically pagan; it is historically "essentially a war organization," and in our time has "risen to greater and greater power over the life and

[41]

death of its citizens." It as a rule "acknowledges no other end than to increase its power and to protect its own interests." [17] Between states morality is not the basis of cooperation, only "etiquette"; for politics, as Lester Ward once said, is still in the Stone Age. In the last two generations women, education and labor have been largely lost to Christianity, women becoming "increasingly body-minded," education devoted to "materialistic achievements," and the "mass of our laboring population" forsaking the church.[18] Even Christianity—or the Christian church—"has adapted itself to the pagan customs of society," having concentrated on "theological doctrines" instead of on the "teaching" of Christ.[19] Ellwood quotes with approval the judgment of E. Stanley Jones: "Most of Christianity has not yet moved into the New Testament. It is pre-Christian and sub-Christian." [20]

Ellwood, standing fully within the social gospel tradition, demands nothing short of a completely Christianized society and civilization. In 1922 he urged the achievement of a Christian economic order. Our economy must be "an ideal order in which the divine will is realized"; and it is the duty of all true Christians "to make the realization of such an order a prime object of the practical religious life." [21] In italics he writes: "For the equalizing of opportunity is of the very essence of a democratic, Christian organization of the economic life." [22] Jesus spoke of "human values" as the aim of social life; and hence an economy may be organized to achieve such values. In regard to this, Ellwood asserts in a remarkable passage: "We have sketched no impossible utopia but only the goal towards which the best economic thinking in our civilization is moving," a type of thinking emphasizing "human values first," "economic obligations rather than economic rights," maximized "cooperation, equal opportunity, and private wealth as a trust held for public good." [23] In 1940, undaunted by world depressions and world wars, he charges American business men to become "followers of Christ," to substitute social service for profit-seeking, and to make business enterprise "conform to the teachings of Christ." [24] "The whole field of business and industry, quite as much as education," he declared, "should evidently become a field of redemption by the Christian Church." [25]

[42]

Governments too must become spiritual, abandoning imperialism, abolishing force and war, with exploitation in domestic affairs and international relations disappearing. "We need a political life built upon a different principle than power as the end, and which shall use different methods than fear and force. Goodwill should replace fear, and understanding should take the place of force." [26] In the same context Ellwood declares that "we need a politics which will recognize the service of humanity as its end." In Chapter IV of *Man's Social Destiny,* entitled "The Future of Government," the sociologist warns that it is "impossible to perfect our social culture unless we perfect government." He observes that in the last twenty-five years (he is writing in 1929) the world seems politically to have "retrograded," two-thirds of the population which in 1918 professed democracy having since repudiated it "without any expressions of regret." [27] Government has oscillated between oppression and "anarchism," always living by the "ethics of war" instead of by the "social welfare conception of government." In our day we have seen, since World War No. 1, autocratic governments stealing the idea of welfare, thus presenting new dangers to American democracy.[28] Thus we are faced with the democratic and Christian challenge to set up a government which will provide for the education of all classes, elimination of poverty, the creation of a minimum standard of living for all men, a drastic redistribution of wealth and an equalization of opportunity throughout the population.[29]

In his later work, written in 1940, Ellwood is hardly less idealistic in regard to the aims and possibilities of political activity. While he professes to avoid a "dogmatic pacifism," and to prove that armies and navies as "police forces" are in accord with "Christ's teachings," he demands a "Christian civilization" based on an "ethics of love." Although nations are not equals, they must live like families, granting all the "same rights, the same protection, under a law governing international relations." The objective is a perfect, peaceful, cooperative, democratic Christian commonwealth world-wide in extent. "If the world," he says, "is the subject of redemption, then the nations have as much of an obligation to help one another in all peaceful activities, in all activities which tend to build up a Kingdom of God among men, as individuals have." [30]

We should note that throughout Ellwood's writings, despite his frequent discussions of international affairs, his occasional tirades against the foreign "isms," and his numerous appeals on behalf of democracy, there is virtually no appreciation of the depth and cultural significance of the political upheavals of our time. His reactions to democracy and the totalitarianisms of Europe are extremely naive, the Fascist and Marxist movements meaning for him only an ignorant malicious repudiation of democratic structures and the unnecessary use of weapons of force over the national populations. Hence he offers no sympathetic interpretations of fascism, communism, socialism or capitalism, presenting only a series of more or less negative, dogmatic reactions.*

He shows how misleading is his economic thinking by holding up on the one hand an extraordinarily utopian democratic ideal virtually equivalent to a Kingdom of God or universal brotherhood on earth, while at the same time giving some striking defenses of the most undemocratic traditions in American life, including unrestricted private property, class divisions, and "social reward" based on what he calls the "ethical legitimacy of interest." True, he attacks in rather wholesale fashion ruthless profit-seeking, the evils of inheritance laws, the "highly unscientific" character of modern capitalism (and of "communistic socialism"), class strife, ridiculous luxuries, the gambling spirit, the menace of unemployment, maldistribution of wealth, and the anti-Christian ethos which expresses itself in "the boldest selfishness, greed and inconsiderateness of others." [31]

At the same time, possessed with the magic of a curiously flexuous logic, he asserts that communism "is impossible in civilized society," that "idealistic morality" is based on private property, that "collective measures" for social security interfere with individual liberty and with the power to look after one's own "welfare and rights." He concludes that it is "absurd" to regard as impossible a "Christian social order or a cooperative commonwealth" merely because of

* Human mentalities present bewildering patterns. A man like E. Stanley Jones, for instance, though only an evangelist with no pretense to breadth of learning or academic refinement, evidently possesses a more penetrating grasp of the historical significance of the political revolutions of our time than does a learned sociologist like Ellwood.

[44]

the "impossibility of the abolition of classes, or because of the primary necessity in economic life of paying attention to production, or because of the impossibility of large groups safeguarding completely the rights and welfare of their individual members without private property and individual liberty." [32] In the context where this quoted passage is found one runs across the intriguing but treacherous notion that despite all the shortcomings and limitations of the existing economy a cooperative brotherhood is possible "because cooperation is more dependent upon inner attitudes and ideals than upon external forms and machinery." *

Turning aside from a consideration of the sociologist's blanket attack upon existing institutional patterns, and from the brief preliminary observation concerning his criticisms, we may look more closely at the positive aspects of his thinking. Perhaps the central plea running throughout Ellwood's lectures and books is the plea for a social or socialized religion. It is equally appropriate, however, since he is extremely enamored of science and its spirit and methodology, to designate his body of ideas as the result of a quest for a Christian Sociology or a Christian Social Science. In this respect too he continues the social gospel tradition, standing in the general line of succession running from Stephen Colwell to Henry George and Richard T. Ely, all of whom, incidentally, were laymen and Christian social scientists.†

Ellwood is an apostle for the cooperation or union of social science

* In *The World's Need of Christ* (pp. 134–36), after pleading for the "socialization of property," he turns with a surprising attack on socialization, having great concern to show that "legal ownership by the community does not necessarily promote a Christian state of society," since legal ownership is "relatively unimportant as compared to the spirit which determines the use of property."

† Henry George is generally regarded as a towering figure, as one of the daringly original minds in the history of social thought, while Ellwood seems least of the four to be an intellectual trail blazer. The latter's *A History of Social Philosophy*, 1938, although a valuable and very readable volume showing catholic interests and wide reading in many of the world's great classics, is quite feeble in its critical quality, to say nothing of the total absence of a constructive original social theory. His recent employment of Sorokin's speculations illustrates the manner in which he simply takes over phrases or ideas and uses them as elaborate texts for moralizing and philosophizing.

[45]

and religion. In the Preface to *The Reconstruction of Religion* one finds this opening sentence: "In previous works the author has repeatedly said: 'One of the greatest social needs of the present is a religion adapted to the requirements of modern life and in harmony with modern science.'" He continues here by claiming that the religion needed by the modern world is a "more rational, revitalized, socialized Christianity," and boasts of his agreement with a certain "eminent leader of Anglo-American" religious thought who said that when Christianity became completely scientific it would "bring about the Millennium." Although religion is not itself science, enlightened Christianity and enlightened social science are one in "conclusions." He carries as a sort of motto for this book—which incidentally is subtitled "A Sociological View"—two quotations respectively from Frederic Harrison's *The Meaning of History* and *The Creed of a Layman,* both quotations expressing perfectly the demand for a socialized, humanized, ethicized faith.

In 1923 he published his *Christianity and Social Science* which fairly bursts with almost boundless confidence in the benign results of an alliance between religion and sociology. In the initial chapter he hails the imminence of a new great culture synthesis, a fresh "synthesis of aspiration with knowledge" which would truly redeem mankind. Just the year preceding he had prophesied that we stand on the brink of a New Reformation "besides which the Protestant Reformation will seem insignificant." [33] When we "boldly harness together our science and our religion," and with this fusion of knowledge and aspiration "seek to control public opinion and social conditions," we shall "turn back the flood of barbarism that now threatens our civilization." Indeed, it would be possible "to modify the whole complex of our social life, or our civilization, within the comparatively short space of one or two generations." [34] In Chapter VI of *Man's Social Destiny,* titled "The Future of Religion," our social scientist again pleads for a humanized faith, pointing out the "cultural utility of religion." He describes a "developed religion," in harmony with a "sound science" which believes in God, Jesus, immortality and sin, a religion expressing itself in a church devoted "to the education of the nobler emotions, the development of pity, sympathy, and love, not limited by the barriers of class, nation, or race, but as wide as humanity itself." [35] Again he affirms confidently that "the teachings of Christ regarding the conduct of persons in society doubtless need to be corroborated by the scientific study of human relations," and that a "thoroughly humanized sociology would be a Christian sociology, in the sense that there would be little or no conflict between it and the teaching of Christ." [36] He assures us that a "Christian sociology" is not based on "previously accepted Christian principles" but verified by "independent investigation"; hence "both religion and science need only to be humanized in order to find that they are both working for the same end—the redemption of man." [37]

Observe that when he pleads for a "social" or "socialized" religion Ellwood is referring to a non-theological, non-ecclesiastical faith. He is quite impatient with dogmas and creeds and church systems of every description, though he remarks casually that sociology will not be a "substitute for theology," but will become the ally of "scientific theology"—scientific theology for him, of course, being a humanized ethics based partly on a few "principles" abstracted from the New Testament. He never tires of hurling his darts at outmoded "doctrines," while at the same time paying his most profound respects to the immortal "teachings of Jesus." He declares in italics: "The religious problem of our day . . . is not a problem in metaphysics or theology; it is a problem in the practical values of human living." [38] He further declares that "original Christianity, that is to say the teachings of Jesus, had but little theology in it." [39]

In instructing us about the fundamental nature of religion, he reminds us that what it seeks is social progress and universal moral ideals; that it is an agency of social control; that it indeed seeks "spiritual" values in contrast to "material" ones. But, let us "distinguish religion from theology on the one hand and ecclesiastical organization on the other"; for although "religions always imply metaphysical or theological beliefs of some sort, no *specific* theological belief is an essential part of religion." [40] In this volume he devotes a chapter to the exclusive task of describing the nature of his proposed revolutionary faith,[41] a faith which turns out to be a naturalistic, scientific "religion of humanity" minus the Comtean embellishments, but having to its dubious credit, be it said, a kindly disposition toward the ideas of God, immortality, sin, salvation and the "principles" of

[47]

love and service taught by Jesus. In his more recent book, *The World's Need of Christ,* he calls a halt to the cultural disintegration of our civilization, declaring that the world paganism is due in part to the church's refusal to "imitate" the Master—a disloyalty which expressed itself "during the last dozen years" in an increasing emphasis on theology rather than on "the practical teachings of Christ." The whole civilized world must "imitate" Christ, he asserts. For its salvation it must turn back to the wonderful master mind whom even Professor Simkhovitch, in admiration of his "intellectual grandeur," ranks as a "greater than Aristotle." [42]

One cannot appreciate, however, this "sociological" approach to the nature of religion without keeping in mind the fundamental outlook of the expositor, namely his overwhelming passion for cultural progress and his deep desire to utilize every resource, including Christianity, as an instrument for social change. His "social religion" has virtually no other value save as a tool for the coming new civilization. Chapter I of *The Reconstruction of Religion* is given the title "The Religious Revolution." Here he remarks in a footnote (p. 2): "The reader will note that the phrase 'religious revolution' is used in this book like the phrase 'industrial revolution,' not to indicate a violent change, but a great transformation. The Protestant Reformation was a religious revolution in this sense." "Unless customs, institutions, and social conditions are made Christian," he warns, "we cannot expect that they will produce Christlike characters in men and women, nor stable and harmonious relations between groups." [43] Again, "our science, our education, and our government can do much to help correct this lag in our spiritual development. But in the main this must be done, if done at all, by religion and the church." [44] Although in *The World's Need of Christ* he remarks that the "essence of Christianity" is in "the following and imitation of Christ" and that the "natural man" is a "creature of impulses and emotions, for the most part self-centered," he is still convinced that man's redemption is "within himself" and that "imitation of Christ" is not self-renunciation or world flight, but a quasi-legalistic acceptance and practice of Jesus' "teachings" and "pattern of life" in such a manner as to lead to an earthly utopia. His exclusive interest here, as in his previous works, is in "the Christian reconstruction of our civilization."

[48]

Ellwood is an unshaken apostle of social progress in the fullest sense of the social gospel tradition. One is possessed of an embarrassing plethora of illustrative materials in his writings.[45] No page references are given in regard to *Man's Social Destiny*, a series of lectures delivered in 1929 at Vanderbilt University. The reason is that the whole volume is in itself a glorious paean to the Coming New Age of Man. Dean O. E. Brown of the Vanderbilt University School of Religion in his Preface to the book hailed the "prophetic voice" of Dr. Ellwood whose lectures radiate "a much-needed Christian optimism—an optimism tested in the fires of sincere scientific criticism and justified in the light of life's best-accredited realities." There is a bit of irony in the fact that this book should have been published in 1929, and that the kind Dean Brown should have underscored its "exceptional timeliness and abiding value."

History sometimes seems to ignore our most cherished prophecies. Ellwood gave as his opening Vanderbilt lecture in 1929 a strong discourse on the subject, "Present Social Pessimism," uttering the challenge: "Let us face this social pessimism, examine the facts, and then see if our knowledge of human history and human society helps us to see our way through the tangled affairs of our world to the probability of a better and happier future." He then marshals before him for rebuke gloomy utterances from European and American prophets of doom, among them M. Paul Gaultier and M. Julien Benda of France, F. C. S. Schiller of Oxford University, John Erskine, C. E. Ayres, Raymond B. Fosdick and Harry F. Ward of the United States. To be sure he admits that these dark observations "must be taken into account in prognosticating the future" and that "the international and interracial situation are both very clouded." Despite the fact that "Christ's ideals have not yet won out," nevertheless "the world has been moving, even though with interruptions, toward these ideals." Moreover, there abides the conviction that there are "scientific grounds for our faith in the possibility and probability of a better human world, in the realization of freedom, justice, and love in human relations." He then announces that in succeeding lectures he will give in more detail the "scientific" grounds for social optimism. He discusses respectively "the resources of mankind," "the future of science," "the future of government," and the future of education and of religion, in five separate lectures. The world since 1929 renders unnecessary any commentary on his belief at the time that the church "is even now arriving" and that "the light of truth is breaking everywhere in our world."

In 1940, at the height of the universal conflagration which was preceded by a world depression, the rise of totalitarianism and the destruction of the League of Nations, our sociologist published *The World's Need of Christ,* dedicated "To The True Followers of Christ Everywhere." His lyrics to progress were withdrawn, his suspicions of the "natural man" proclaimed, his disillusionment with Rousseauism, Nietzscheanism, and Freudianism voiced, while the hero of the drama, Auguste Comte, was replaced by the gloomy prophet of a disintegrating sensate culture, P. A. Sorokin. Ellwood in this volume denounces the tendency to exalt natural goodness and "natural forces" when the need is for a real individual "conversion" and for a civilization determined on the "imitation of Christ." Religious education and psychology must again become "Christ-centered," he charges, while "all the great spiritual leaders and heroes" must be honored instead of the playboy and soldier "types." Christians cannot survive in an unchristian society, and hence even groups must imitate Christ, at least in spirit. Whether in "science and philosophy," economic activity, domestic politics, international relations or church life—indeed in all of these—the call comes to create a "Christian culture." "We should all ask ourselves," he challenges, "whether we have carried the Christ-spirit into all our human relations, and whether we have laid our life work at the foot of the cross as our contribution to the building of Christ's Kingdom in this world." [46]

Now at first glance it appears that our spokesman for cultural progress has been shocked into radical disillusionment; but far from it. He finds the root trouble in such matters as the church's blind exaltation of traditional dogma, a widespread lack of appreciation for a "specific, critical examination of Christ's social teachings," [47] the tendency to substitute a "God-centered" religion for a "Christ-centered" one, an inveterate love of Hobbism, the inadequate conversion of ecclesiastical leadership, a general failure to perceive the incompatibility between Christianity and modern culture, the materialistic preoccupations of science, the failure of the church to promote science, and particularly a "social ignorance which envelops our human world." He even drops the suggestion that in the last century "a host of leaders in almost every branch of the church began to demand a return to Christ and to active building of the Kingdom of God among men"; and that all this might have been the beginning of the ideal Christian Age save that World War No. 1 "brought a sudden halt to this hopeful movement." [48] True, "sensate" civilization has failed; but "a Christian culture is not impossible for the mass of mankind, even though the natural man fights against it; for all culture is learned and the possibilities of human learning are far from exhausted." Though paganism is easier, the "Christian way of life may be learned by the mass of men." [49]

In short, though in recent years somewhat disturbed and not a little puzzled, Ellwood had an unreconstructed confidence in the unlimited possibilities of human nature. His early works of course are built entirely upon the presumption that with social science, a humanized Christianity and more modern techniques in religious education men, despite the existence of a "semi-pagan civilization," can build an earthly utopia, a Kingdom of God in this world, within a generation or two. The principal tool in this "reconstruction" of civilization, in this "New Reformation," should be a social religion or Christian social science, since the one basic need of the world is instruction in the simple truths of the gospel and in the use of scientific method. In his later books this fundamental conviction persists. In *A History of Social Philosophy* (1938) he argues that "man is an animal, not only built to live by learning, but built to live by learning from his fellow creatures." "All human institutions," he continues, "and nearly all interactions between civilized human beings, are learned adjustments, derived for the most part from the general culture of the group. This is the cultural view of human society that is revolutionizing the social sciences." [50] Thus as a sociologist he is "more interested in the cultural modifications brought about in man's natural tendencies and animal impulses than he is in the limits that these organic conditions impose." [51] He is ready therefore to refute those "who claim, for example, that war and

[51]

military systems cannot be abandoned by civilized nations through the change of their culture and social traditions"; and to throw "a considerable burden of proof upon those who claim that customs and institutions cannot be changed." [52] Having surveyed all the great social philosophies of the world, he prefers the outlook of Lester F. Ward who "saw the possibilities involved in the process of human social development, and in thus laying down the foundations of a scientific, an educational, and a political meliorism, he gave us a sounder, more enduring social philosophy." [53]

Ellwood possesses an ideal of social reformism, even if he did remark once in italics that he demands "not so much the reformation of human society" as the "transformation of human society into a Kingdom of God." [54] Despite his numerous strictures on the capitalist ethos dominating American life, and his branding of American capitalism as "ruthless, unregulated business," he merely wavers between a recommendation of "cooperative enterprises" and an evangelistic appeal to industrialists to follow the service ideal. He stands ready to build his "democratic Christian organization of society" upon all the present inequalities, with individuals voluntarily sacrificing for each other; for the "social wisdom of Christ" is the spirit of "conferring mutual benefits upon one another." [55] He issues an appeal to business to become "devoted to the redemption of mankind," for after all it "might pay modern capitalism to become radically Christian!"

He reveals an extremely hopeful attitude toward institutional development and toward the potential blessings of "love" and "social service." He assures the church that it could readily and almost immediately "reconstruct" civilization if it should attack and combat "sensate elements in society," and then go on to the two-fold task of teaching universal goodwill and of organizing "enthusiasm for the Christian cause among its members." [56] He pleads for "social justice," insisting upon the "family pattern as the only pattern which will work in human relations in the long run."

Though possessing a pronounced social gospel outlook Ellwood advocates a type of reformism devoid of any concern for economic or political strategies. All his tirades against existing evil structures appear to be largely rhetorical and sentimental, since he does not really believe in a Kingdom of God revolution, as does E. Stanley Jones. On some occasions he hails the Scandinavian cooperative movement as the symbol of a dawning new day; but this too turns out to be more of an illustration for a sociological sermon than of belief that the Kingdom is really at hand. Actually he is exclusively concerned about "research in harmonizing human relations." Academic religious sociology is his *open sesame* to the coming revolution. Strangely enough, he dismisses most of the social philosophers of the world as having "sought for some single key to unlock the mystery of human relations and human development." [57] But he himself offers the simplest of such keys—a Christian social science!

4

Religious-Democratic Reformism: Francis J. McConnell

IN A BRIEF ESSAY one writes with some misgivings about a man like Francis J. McConnell, for his interests and activities have been very numerous and his labors have covered many areas of public life, local, national and international. Even his academic interests are quite many-sided, touching among other things technical theological problems, speculations in politics and economics, and special questions about public opinion, propaganda, democratic organization, the role of law in society, human incentives, and techniques of social change. He is a man who is at once churchman, citizen, educator, administrator, writer, theologian, and democrat in the best sense of this much-abused term. Ever since his election in 1912 to the bishopric in the Methodist Episcopal Church he has employed the advantages of his office in such a fashion as to exercise enormous influence on behalf of the various liberal movements of our generation.

Just to list his books, articles, and connections is in itself significantly to characterize the bishop. He has been president at one time or another of the following (among others): De Pauw University, the Federal Council of the Churches of Christ in America, the Methodist Federation for Social Service, the American Association for Social Security, the World Fellowship of Faiths, the Religious Education Association, and the People's Lobby. Also he served as chairman of the Commission of the Interchurch World Movement investigating the steel strike of 1919, and as a member of various boards and commissions dealing with work in foreign lands, notably in Latin America and China. His innumerable articles and more than two dozen books appear in the course of a unique career of public service extending over a period of more than forty years. During this time he also gave courses of lectures at the Wesleyan University, the universities of Illinois and of Southern California, the Pacific School of Religion, Vanderbilt, De Pauw, Northwestern and Southern Methodist universities. In 1930 he gave the Lyman Beecher Lectures at Yale, and in 1931 the Barrows Lectures in India. Important public matters with which he has concerned himself touch civil rights, labor organization, social security, economic and political reforms, international agreements, race relations, world peace plans, the missionary enterprise, church unity programs, religious education and theological reconstruction. A fitting tribute was paid him as churchman, scholar, and world citizen when in 1937 a volume of essays edited by H. F. Rall was dedicated to him under the title of *Religion and Public Affairs!* [1]

Bishop McConnell represents a significant aspect of Protestant social thought, not merely because of his own tremendous personal influence, but also because his manner of approach to current problems is typical of a widespread tendency running through the whole history of American liberal Christianity. He follows faithfully in the social gospel tradition as a rebel against the status quo, as an advocate of numerous and sundry reforms, as a champion of Christian idealism in its application to democracy, as an opponent of otherworldly religion in all its forms, as a herald of a humanized faith, and as an earnest believer in the coming Kingdom on earth. But he gives no positive, constructive, systematic body of doctrine in regard to political or economic matters. There is hardly a single concept, or set of concepts, or even a single line of attack around which his views may be organized or by which they may be adequately described. He possesses no doctrinaire socialism, no militant pacifism, no Marxian theoretics, no Kingdom of God utopianism, no passion for a Christian sociology, economics or politics. His is a more or less negative, piecemeal criticism which tends to apply

[55]

Christian principles and insights in *ad hoc* fashion to any and all problems demanding attention.

For more than a quarter-century McConnell has brought forth a general indictment of the modern social order, although his attack has not been characterized by sustained revolutionary ardor nor by any conscious repudiation of capitalist culture as such. For the most part he has singled out specific areas of evil, describing vividly maladjustments or "unchristian" practices and institutions and often suggesting remedies. In volume after volume (though without pretense at orderly arrangements) he offers criticism in regard to virtually every major social ill in modern civilization.*

He is strongly against "secularization and paganization of industry," as well as against "virtual deification of worldly success." [2] We are in great need of a new economic order because among other things the worker needs to work "for the work's own sake," and because we can never set forth a convincing Christianity "until there is economic freedom for men in this positive degree." [3] Indeed, we are compelled to "change our system" in order that laborers may feel themselves working for "an entire community of men" rather than for a "limited number of private owners planning chiefly for their own profit." [4] He denounces the prevalence of the war spirit in our culture, dishonest diplomacy, imperialism, nationalism, racism and economic exploitation among the so-called backward peoples and countries. "It requires only the slightest acquaintance with current political conditions today," he charges, "to see that fear rules the capitals of the Christian nations." [5] As for race superiority, it is the greatest single hindrance to the spread of world Christianity.[6] With the rise of fascism we see disorder everywhere. We are in gravest danger, for a "world utterly chaotic without any fixed rules or procedure is no world at all." [7] Among the worst evils is the fact that our statesmen are not "farsighted," but in tackling world issues merely act "from day to day," thus unintelligently exerting "incalculable influence on the times ahead." [8] Throughout the nineteenth century we have

---

* The rather non-committal character of much of his literary effort is due in part no doubt to the fact that he often wrote what amounts to handbooks under the auspices of various boards or other sponsoring groups. Cf. for instance his *Christian Materialism* and *The Church After the War*.

been preaching "ideals" but refusing to see the facts "as they are," aggression arising continually (especially on the part of Germany) while the "non-Germanic peoples" did not take the threat seriously.[9]

In his sharp indictment of modern society McConnell does not spare the church and Christianity generally. In an early work he brands the church as a mere "relief agency," not coming to "grips with socialism" and thus not giving sufficient "help in the democratic movement." [10] Western Christianity, he asserts in reference to the missionary enterprise, has not recognized "the human claims of non-Christian peoples," it being "a sad commentary on our Christianity" that we did not realize that Orientals were entitled to such human rights until the "so-called heathen peoples had themselves insisted upon" them.[11] Rejecting the laissez-faire attitude toward "mechanical progress" with its attendant intolerable unemployment, he cries out against the "paganism of Christendom which talks about inevitabilities in modern civilization to which we must submit." [12] In *Christianity and Coercion,*[13] although he defends and explains the failings of the church, he acknowledges that "there is much warrant" for the loss of "popular hold by the church," for "depleted congregations," indifference to "high themes" and for the failure of "evangelistic campaigns." A suspicion of the social power of ecclesiastical authorities is expressed: "The verdict of historical research would, I think, have to be that the Church, or the churches, have never yet reached the understanding of themselves or of Christianity which would make it safe to intrust powers of physical coercion to them." [14] There is the further regret that the "corporate forces of the Church are so often on the side of social repression," the leaders too often being "prone to think of themselves as set to guard something."

It may be said at this juncture, however, that Bishop McConnell does not attack the church with the sharpness and the uncompromising righteous fury of most social gospel writers expounded in these pages. Indeed, he is more inclined to defend Christianity and to explain its functions than he is to utter strictures against it. In the context of most of the passages where negative criticisms are offered one finds defenses, explanations, carefully phrased justifications. After expressing doubts as to the advisability of making re-

[57]

ligion a coercive political or police force, he then glorifies the "true Church as a Blessed Community." [15] We must all return to the Church, he declares, "as a body in society, playing its part as a member of society." In fact, when they are members of the church, "a group of believers whose words and deeds, when they are acting together may move in a far higher realm than when the individuals act separately." [16] Even if it is worthy of criticism, the church is highly critical of itself: "There is not any other institution of society which seems more willing to have its faults pointed out than is the Church." *

Returning to the general attack on the social order, it is noteworthy that the bishop is extremely dissatisfied with the existing capitalist system. In many places his position is strongly anti-capitalist, indeed at times on the borders of genuine socialism. Our economy is one in which capital "is so largely the tools of production, that the working classes, with no title to the tools with which they work, are dependent on the owners of the tools to a degree which is undemocratic and anti-social." [17] In a competitive system there are "masses of manufactures" which cannot be disposed of; there is a "slowing down, with consequent unemployment and general distress." Hence "with all our scientific knowledge, we have not organized society on a sound enough basis to insure it against being smothered by its own product." "This is the weak spot in our so-called Christian civilization." [18] If we simply look at the "material values themselves," leaving out reference to "ideals," what argument have we "for the duty of spreading a material civilization of the type which has arisen in so many nominally Christian lands?" Capitalism is selfish, inefficient, exploiting. In referring to a book written by Sir Sidney Oliver, entitled *White Capital and Colored Labor,* the

* *Christianity and Coercion* (Cokesbury Press, 1933), p. 122. Elsewhere McConnell gives an almost fantastically rosy view of the church as a thoroughly democratic system—as a "church of the people, by the people, for the people." *Democratic Christianity,* Chapter II. This was written in 1919. Though in later books he has chastened his language somewhat, the genial, kindly, apologetic attitude toward ecclesiastical religion persists. See, for instance, *The Church After the War* (Chapter IV, titled "Christian Democracy"), where he defends and idealizes American denominationalism and proclaims the coming of a "global body of religion."

bishop remarks: "Why should the black man care for more than enough to eat? What advantage is there for him in the capitalistic virtue of thrift? What virtue is there in a thrift which produces more than the Negro gets any benefit from? Labor as hard as he may, the disproportionate share of his product goes to white men." There is much opposition to our religion in foreign countries because "scores and hundreds identify Christianity with aggressive Western capitalism." In *Christianity and Coercion* a complaint is made that "in competition for markets or for individual jobs . . . the stakes are too high" (p. 82); that newspapers are generally regarded by labor as "tools of the employing and possessing groups" (p. 36 f); that the great danger in America is not proletarian revolution but a moneyed dictatorship of the fascist type (p. 43).[19]

There are innumerable strictures on nationalism, imperialism and the war system, which evils are regarded frequently as inevitable by-products of capitalism and the industrial revolution. In *Human Needs and World Christianity,* he accuses this western "Christian" industrialization with being unfit to reform the tropics (pp. 60 f., 65), with seizing of resources and with exploitation of labor (pp. 66–67), with arousing anti-Christian forces in places like China, India, Japan, and Mexico (pp. 121, 131 ff). Criticisms are leveled at the historic policies of industrial nations in Africa, Mexico and the Far East, including their application of "humanity's right of eminent domain," which principle "was relied upon to justify barbarities on the part of the United States in the Philippines, to cite a single instance." * Bishop McConnell's position on socialism or on radical economic theories in general is difficult to state and evaluate. In his writings there are several isolated expressions of admiration for socialism (even for Marx himself), some passages openly prophesying the triumph of socialism. In *Democratic Christianity* there are three sections (in Chapter III) titled respectively "Socialism," "The Dogmatism of Socialism," and "The British Labor Party." Here Karl

---

* *Christianity and Coercion,* pp. 26–27. Yet in *The Church After the War* (pp. 40–44) he points out the blessings of Christian imperialism, saying that England stumbled on her empire gradually, that basically imperialism is not "sin" but "self-preservation and self-expansion," as was true of the purpose of ancient Rome and "all empires since."

Marx is hailed as a mighty pioneer, an intellectual revolutionary in social theory, like Kant in philosophy and Darwin in science. The usual objections to socialism are recounted, namely, that it is atheistic, anarchistic and immoral; but, says McConnell, all these charges are largely untrue. Those who raise such objections, he retorts, "reveal at once that they have not kept pace with socialistic discussions." *
In *Human Needs and World Christianity,* he remarks; "If China, for example, is indeed just emerging from medievalism, she ought to have a chance at a Christianity which teaches the social control of all agencies of production in the name of the inviolable sacredness of individuals." [20] Again, in regard to railways of India and Egypt, "enterprises like these must be socially carried through in the name of the Christian ideal of humanity." [21]

Sometimes McConnell merely advocates a policy of peaceful socialization of industry; at other times he sees an evolution toward collectivism now in process within the framework of capitalism. "We are all agreed that the present social order has to give way to something more cooperative, not stopping short of the social ownership of the greater means of production, or a social control that comes virtually to the same end." [22] He is not favorably disposed toward the "parlor" revolutionists on the one hand or the militant critics of Sovietism on the other. He would justify both the French and Russian revolutions, noting especially that Czarism was far worse than Bolshevist revolution. Besides socialism is coming anyway; and fundamentally it is nothing to be alarmed about. Even "a road is a bit of socialism." [23] He suggests that economic structures should be so reordered as to "eliminate from the sphere of competition altogether the struggle for elemental needs." [24]

In the article in Page (below, note 24) McConnell gives an excellent illustration of his type of criticism and reasoning. He issues tirades against capitalism, while regarding "a limited private capitalism" as possible and desirable. He advocates socialism, yet is rather suspicious of it. One major point emphasized here, of course, is that co-operation as an incentive is more powerful as an economic force

* In the same context he attacks socialism, particularly its dogma about interest and its prejudice toward capitalists. In fact, socialism "deals in self-evident certainties which are not sun-clear when closely examined." *Ibid.,* p. 51.

than competition. He inveighs against workers' insecurity, implying that the working class is becoming ever more restless against a system which dooms them to fear, wage-slavery, low standards of living, unemployment and industrial oligarchy. He says that we need more effective leadership in "social engineering," a less materialistic philosophy (which is strengthened among lower classes by poverty), and even a minimum of $6,000 for a family of five so as "to break the bondage of thwarting overdependence upon matter." He warns against the danger of certain types of labor-management cooperation; while on the other hand pleading not for direct economic democracy but for a responsible leadership of experts who possess a "conscientious feeling of trusteeship." The main trouble is that managers, engineers and directors do not lead "unselfishly and effectively." Finally, competition for the "fundamental basic necessities" should be abolished and "competition in other fields" increased.

Notice carefully that in this article McConnell's analysis virtually presupposes the necessity and desirability of a basically new social order other than competitive capitalism. He repeatedly makes reference to an order which is "predominantly co-operative" as contrasted with an undesirable one "predominantly competitive." His argument is that human nature is wrongly viewed in the assumptions of capitalism, for men would be encouraged to do more, even in industrial production, if the spirit of co-operation prevailed throughout the economy. As we have indicated, he suggests that the supply of the basic necessities of life be removed from the sphere of competition altogether, and that large-scale industry be put under the control of unselfish expert management subject to democratic controls. Nonetheless his analysis involves only a piecemeal criticism of undesirable elements and aspects of the existing capitalist order without a clear-cut suggestion that genuine socialism of any kind is desirable.

McConnell seems to waver between a compromising, non-violent democratic reformism and an out-and-out socialism. Without doubt he rejects laissez-faire capitalism in favor of some kind of controlled economy. Occasionally an approach is made toward a genuine collectivism which presumably is evolving by the inherent development of large-scale enterprise, accompanied with the gradual assumption by government of new economic functions. At other times he appears

[61]

to place his trust in the increasing democratization and Christianization of industry without the necessity of a radical shift in economic
power, at least not of the kind of shift taken for granted in socialist
theory. His conviction is that social change of whatever degree may
be accomplished by non-violent, democratic means, though he takes
for granted that coercion (which is not the same as "force" or "threat
of force") will be necessary. Incidentally his position on coercion is
just as confusing as it is on socialism. He eschews all violence, defends pacifism as applied to the peace-war question—calling the position of the "absolutist conscientious objector" the "most Christian
stand on the war question"—and spiritualizes force by approving of
the "coercion of law," "intellectual compulsion" and "social pressure." The church is urged to apply only the "higher coercions," that
is, "intellectual and moral magnetism." [25] Hence there is no overt endorsement of the aims and tactics of any particular socialist school,
nor yet any direct repudiation of socialist objectives or techniques.

In his *Christian Materialism* (1936) we have a statement full of
denunciations of the basic ills in capitalism, a literary sermon (or
an elaborate Sunday School lesson, if the reader so prefers) delivered
against both the central ethos of capitalism and all its attendant evil
products in social life. McConnell demands that in every business
deal there be three gainers—buyer, seller and society—contending
that since neither capitalist nor wage-earner thinks "much about
public welfare, society has to stand firmly for the third gainer to every
bargain—society itself" (p. 6). Through our history the "mass of
American people" subscribed to the principle of "every man for himself and the devil take the hindmost," there being always on hand
"unscrupulous leaders" taking advantage of such economic "chaos"
(p. 7). Society, he says, is the true "creator of values" and thus has
a right to take such values, for it would be "impracticable" to draw
up a list of good, morally responsible businesses worthy of invest-
ments for Christians (p. 22). He is alarmed at the "spectacle" that
between October, 1929, and January, 1935, there were no bank failures
in England and only one or two in Canada while there were 2,000
in the United States (p. 31). He acknowledges that when Christian
pastors seek to administer to individuals "in the great cities" they
finally "come up against the huge corporative forces as against a

stone wall (p. 32 f.). The conclusion is drawn that "there must be a planned society" (p. 42). The greater productive agencies, though they are already moving in the direction of socialization, must be taken "under social control, if not ownership, at the earliest practicable date" (p. 63).

Now all the ideas expressed in the preceding paragraph—and many more strictures on the existing economy could be quoted from the same volume—give the general impression that the critic is really done with the competitive, profit-seeking system. But far from it! His defense of capitalism is just as powerful as his complaint against it. Indeed, the stated purpose of his manual is merely to Christianize capitalism, to show how our inherited pioneer economy may become a "Christian materialism" exercising such control over the getting, spending and giving of money that our scramble for wealth may be guided into "moral and spiritual purposes." The book concludes with a sublime faith: "The material force can become spiritual. Materialism can be converted and sanctified so that through it can be made the revelation of a new creation at hands of the sons of God" (p. 167).

Two other passages illustrate his ambiguous approach when dealing with the problem of economic reconstruction. In *Democratic Christianity* (pp. 48–55) Marx is highly praised, the critics of socialism rebuked, the evils of capitalist emphasis on profits and "unearned" inheritance exposed, and the British Labor Party's platform hailed as an ideal type of "industrial democracy, self-control in the various industries, the nationalization of monopoly value resources." Yet in the same passage socialism is vigorously scored and capitalists are defended as often "being convinced of the inequalities of the present economic system" and as "using their means to bring in a better day." He goes so far as to make the claim that "most socialists today would concede that any man is entitled to all he earns—the full product of his labor in other words—no matter if that should prove to be ten or a hundred or a thousand times as much as another man receives." [26]

In *Christianity and Coercion* he discusses Russia in particular and revolution in general. "It is important," he reminds us here, "not to forget that revolutions may be among the great social blessings."

Both the French and the Russian revolutions "have about them something of the inevitable," although in the case of the latter the "creation of a general will' by force, "by silencing opposition," is not really "democratic." Yet the Bolsheviki were only like a "midwife" who brings the revolution to birth, the figure itself suggesting the "naturalness of the process by which revolutions come into being." Not pleased with coercion, however, McConnell gives a formula for preventing revolutions which, being "profoundly human" and not subject to mere impersonal forces, may be obviated by "going back through the years and stopping whatever tends to depress human values." In this same volume he declares: "We admit the right of revolution in a nation—the right to change its form of government when it thinks it can better itself. That is a long way, however, from conceding that the instruments of change must be violent." But he goes on to say (after justifying revolution) that "the minority is not likely to get wide-scale chance to exercise physical force, and the majority does not need it." [27]

Thus if there is any one thing which could come close to summing up McConnell's ideology it would be his passion for Christian democracy—or as the little volume written at the end of World War No. 1 phrases it in the title, *Democratic Christianity*. In this early book he is looking for a religious utopia which would be born from a marriage between the church and a society becoming increasingly humane, generous, peace-loving and enlightened about human values. Christianity is truly democratic, he boasts, and American denominationalism is "democracy run wild." [28] Autocracy is doomed, and the religio-democratic spirit as revealed in the great war against all forms of autocracy is on the march everywhere. God is now truly in human affairs. Indeed, democracy is but one powerful manifestation of the Christian spirit, as the total society of Christian people is moving toward a "vast democratic organization." [29] In *Public Opinion and Theology* (1920) the Kingdom of God is held up as a democracy of free men (p. 141). Christianity must be humanized, socialized; for "the Christian ideal, at least for the ultimate state of things, is that all earthly forces shall serve the interests of the spiritual life" (p. 83). The "bread-winning processes" must be "so Christianized as to make them the fair field for moral and spiritual judgments" (p. 80). The church's main duty is the proclamation of lofty ideals (pp. 188 ff., 190), for the Kingdom itself is nothing less than the Kingdom of religious truth (pp. 86, 87 ff.).* Even in 1943 McConnell could write that "Christian morality must bring more and more men within the circuit of good will. We have to come back repeatedly to the New Testament ideal of good will which reaches beyond the limits of nation, or of race, or of class, or of sex, or of earthly condition." [30] Again, "we have pretty well learned this lesson [that deeds must express good will] so far as the narrower realm of personal and individual conduct are concerned. The further duty is to sanctify all our activities with a religious purpose." [31]

It would be a simple matter to quote many other passages throughout McConnell's writings on social issues to illustrate the fact that he is a true Christian democrat. Indeed, in his *Humanism and Christianity* (1928) he completely humanizes the church, that is, he virtually eliminates the line between the sacred and the secular.† More than this: he tends to sanctify the secular wherever it presents values to be approved. Whatever contributes any good to civilization is "Christian" and democratic, and the contributor though atheistic is a member of the "body of Christ."

He everywhere reveals a strong confidence in the integrity of established democratic government, in the constitutional basis of our political life, in the ability of the whole people to reach large decisions by rational, peaceful procedures, in the continuing evolution of American public policy in the direction of democratic values and "socialistic" structures, and in the necessity for vigorous criticism of current practices to insure progressive reforms. He seems nonetheless not inclined to take seriously the problem of processes, structures and political forms since he identifies democracy always with certain values or ideals. It is the quest for the good life, the promotion of public welfare, the increasing Christianization of popular sentiment, or respect for the "worth of the individual." Even St. Paul has given

* In *Democratic Christianity* (p. 2) it is said that there is "no irreverence whatsoever in saying that in the end men will everywhere vote for God." Indeed, our world was getting so democratic in 1919 that it was on the verge of voting out the absolutist God and voting in the democratic God!

† Especially in Chapter II titled "The Church and the World."

us the "best picture of Christian democracy" though he probably never heard "of a word suggesting democracy." A hierarchical structure like the Soviet Government or the Catholic Church may be truly democratic "if the hierarchy were deliberately sensitive to and quickly responsive to the mighty currents of the peoples' life." But almost nowhere does he seem to be deeply conscious of the precariousness and instability of so-called peoples' governments and laws, of the ever-present threat of demagogues, of the enormous influence of inertia, tradition and sentiment in social policy, of the immeasurable ingenuity of power groups, particularly wealthy business organizations, to manipulate democratic structures and ideologies in the service of their pet interests.

It is quite illuminating to examine the basis for this extreme democratic faith, in Bishop McConnell's conception of human nature and of man's capacity for effecting institutional changes. Here again the social gospel mind reveals perhaps its central trait, namely, an undisturbed confidence in the goodness, sincerity, reasonableness, and altruism of men, both as individuals and as groups. Consequently, virtually all woes in society are considered as due to ignorance, faulty education, inadequately developed scientific instruments, false theories, and temporarily maladjusted institutional patterns. In 1919 he assumed that the evils in world diplomacy were caused by "obsolescent international doctrines" or by a "creed of international conduct which will one day have to be set aside." [32] Men must simply learn that they are "parts of a divine family," that liberty, equality and fraternity must "win the free assent of men as qualities most truly divine." [33]

In *Public Opinion and Theology* there is the same pronounced intellectualism. The book in fact is written primarily to show that the ideals and beliefs of society are rapidly changing so as to permit the voting in of a brave new world; and McConnell confesses his belief that "in the long run public opinion will settle practically everything in theology" (p. 31). The glorification of a benign public opinion is continued in *Human Needs and World Christianity*.[34] We can show our repentance for the crimes of imperialism, he assures us, "by seeking to build up today a public opinion which will make against any exploitation whatever of the labor of non-Christian peoples by the so-called Christian peoples"; that is, "if we are sincere in our condemnation of their exploiting." We must realize that the "only effective remedy for the evils of the labor problem in Africa is the pressure of an informed American and European public opinion." We can "make Christian workers in every land intelligible to one another" by the impact "of a unified Christian public opinion which must spring from a world-wide Christianity." Again: "There is more sentiment in the world for world organization now than there was among the American colonies for union in 1787." *

The Church After the War (1943) is studded throughout with expressions revealing this genial confidence not only in the comparative simplicity of social problems but also in the good intentions of our Christian "democratic leadership." "If Churchill's advice could have been followed (that is, large amounts of food "rushed into Germany" after World War No. 1) it is at least conceivable that there might not have been a second world war" (p. 25). The duty of the church is to teach "Christian morality" which will "bring more and more men within the circuit of good will," a New Testament "ideal of good will which reaches beyond the limits of nation, or of race, or of class, or of sex, or of earthly condition" (p. 134). Our further duty is simply to sanctify all our institutions "with a religious purpose," for "we have pretty well learned this lesson so far as the narrower realm of personal and individual conduct are concerned" (p. 134).

Men are not bad, not even the "so-called privileged groups"; for we are justified in believing that the fault of such groups "is not necessarily greed or extortion or callousness." [35] Their temptation is merely "the misuse of power," which power of course is "always peril," as Lord Acton pointed out. The industrialists and the masses are not to be judged harshly, for the "people themselves are coming more and more to control their own national possessions and they are coming more and more also to understand the sounder principles of taxation and of the expenditure of public funds." [36] At one place he recalls the socialist indictment of capitalism for its autocracy, hypocrisy, insecurity of workers, and for management's sabotage of

* Note that this last statement is taken from a book copyrighted in 1929, just after the bishop's vision of a coming world Christianity as foreshadowed at the Jerusalem Conference in 1928.

production. But all this bitterness is declared to be unjustified, as due largely to the "workers' state of mind," to a false and an extreme class consciousness akin to "religious mysticism." [37] The bondage of the machine is exaggerated; there are no "iron laws of economics"; industrialists are growing in social consciousness; and the control of industry, as we can see in public roads and water supply systems, "will more and more pass to society as a whole." *

It is quite easy to attain church unity. The churches are not fighting each other like armies! All we need to do is to get rid of certain misconceptions, especially the inability to make "distinction between ends and means," and the habit of making the "organizational features of the Church" an "object of worship." [38] Denominationalism is not bad: "The sincerity of these secessionist believers is as genuine as that of any other group." When "all is said and done, the impulse toward a global body of religion is becoming stronger with the passage of every day." [39] In discussing the question of postwar reconstruction the bishop warns that "we are not to suppose that the heart of man has become desperately wicked or has increased in wickedness at all." Our moral energy has merely been exhausted by the "extraordinary burst of effort in prosecuting the war." [40]

It is no cause for wonder therefore to discover McConnell seeing a coming Christian society in many types of institutional changes and social trends. We have already noted that in his early volume, *Democratic Christianity*, he hailed the imminent arrival of a world-wide democratic-Christian system. This faith is not dimmed appreciably in the later works, whether they were written in the roaring paradise of the twenties, under the shadow of the depression, or during the catastrophic war against totalitarianism. In what he calls "Christian Federalism," that is, in trends toward unity and in democratic practices within ecclesiastical bodies, we see that "the Spirit of Christ is no doubt in the world." [41] Even a monarchy "immediately sensitive to and expressive of popular will" might "conceivably be democratic," for mere organizational forms do not indicate whether "an institution is democratic or not." [42] Democratic England is

---

* *Christianity and Coercion*, pp. 79–81. He turns right around, however, and accuses American workers for not being deeply "class-conscious," but for seeking "profits" and avenues of escape into the employing class. *Ibid.*, pp. 83 f.

ready to grant self-government everywhere.[43] The present wave of one hundred percent patriotism "does not by any means imply that there is a "cult of patriotism," but merely that there are with us "constitutions and laws" pointing to "something beyond themselves." *

Movements for civil rights, public welfare schemes, labor organization, expressions of goodwill or benevolence—all these are signs of a truly triumphant Christianity. "A genuinely Christian program in our social life," he judges, "is that which seeks the support of the old, what we think of as the old-age pension provision, or any well-considered plan of old-age security."[44] Hence the Beveridge Plan was one of the "most ideal" and "most practical expressions of Christianity ever proposed to a nation's legislature."[45] Organized labor today is "running in the direction" of individual worth, a direction "substantially Christian." † Education and promotion of civil rights for Negroes show a cause "unmistakably Christian." In sum, if there are any earthly institutions which cannot be baptized "into the spirit of Christ," then they "have no abiding place in the Christian Kingdom."[46]

We must not overlook the fact that here and there elements of sober skepticism about men and institutions creep into McConnell's expositions. Even in *Democratic Christianity* he acknowledges matter-of-factly that communities of good men (those obsessed with the silly idea of war) may be "socially insane." In one place in the same volume he catches a glimpse of the potentiality of evil in democracy: "Democracy is not necessarily and inherently and irresistibly a good thing in itself," particularly if it becomes "a colossal agency for smothering the voices of the prophets." Again, he sees sinful tendencies in various groups, in organizations which "tend to become conservative" and give the "wirepuller and manipulator his opportunity."[47] Public opinion and sentiments are sometimes irrational or whimsical. Indeed, in one remarkable passage which is far from typical of his social gospel perspective McConnell charges that doc-

---

* *Humanism and Christianity*, p. 35. But here McConnell adds the clause, "though we are not always sure at just what they [the constitutions and laws] do point."

† *Ibid.*, pp. 126 f. Yet labor has, admits the bishop, "no avowed profession of Christian aim."

[69]

trines, philosophies and even scientific theories are "fashionable," are the result of "popularity" in so far as they prevail in a given society.[48] He remarks (casually of course) that "human minds being what they are," it is doubtful if we can really check these intellectual fads until they have run their course. The whole drift of the argument in the context of the last-quoted passages implies that human minds are largely fashion-controlled minds, even the best of them. After arguing strongly that the masses are becoming wiser every day to the glorious advantages of a socialized economy, he spoils a section dealing with the "aims of industry in a Christian community" by an incidental concluding sentence: "It is amazing how many of us still give ourselves to expenditures for display in the hope of recognition by what is called society." [49]

These skeptical observations are, however, a minor feature in the clergyman's outlook. They do not alter the basic character of his approach to human nature and society, namely, an approach which makes central the wisdom, unselfish morality, benevolent intentions and rational social imagination of men in their personal and collective behavior. This assurance which he has in the essential goodness and rationality of men helps to account for his liberalism and democratic social idealism.

5

Christian-Pacifist Socialism:
Kirby Page

KIRBY PAGE is a zealous missionary and a Christian political analyst who has had a dramatic, adventurous career. As a very young man he made excursions into the pastorate, Y.M.C.A. work and into evangelism, with writing always as a consuming interest. During the First World War he was ordained in the Christian Church (1915), served the Y.M.C.A. in Europe (1915–16) and acted as secretary to Sherwood Eddy (1916–18). These responsibilities offered valuable opportunities for travel over the United States, England, France, China, Japan and Korea. After a relatively brief pastorate from 1918 to 1921, he abandoned the life of the ecclesiastic and henceforth became a free lance lecturer, journalist, political agitator, and a world traveller. From 1926 to 1934 he was editor of *The World Tomorrow,* a periodical devoted to pacifism, socialism and "radical" religion. Likewise his rôle in the militantly pacifist Fellowship of Reconciliation has been a major one, including the holding of the position of Vice Chairman. During the quarter century and more since Versailles Kirby Page has written voluminously, publishing in addition to a long list of articles more than two dozen books and about a score of pamphlets.[1]

As journalist, political reformer, socialist, pacifist, and critic, Page is an outstanding protagonist for the social gospel. Throughout his utterances, activities and interests one perceives an undying passion for the application of religious ideas to public issues. The "way of Jesus" is contrasted with the "way of war," or the way of capitalism, or even with the way of the church when the latter becomes the embodiment of barren traditions, outworn culture-patterns and irrelevant theology. In 1929 he set forth an arresting book under the title of *Jesus or Christianity,* in which he sharply contrasts the *religion of Jesus* with the religion known as "Christianity." Traditional Christianity, he declared, has become a "denatured religion" which accepts militarism, nationalism, individualism, racism, and selfish, capitalistic profit-seeking. We must recover the true religion of the Galilean, is the plea, and go forward to build his Kingdom on the earth. The "mind" of Jesus must be understood and his revolutionary ethic applied to modern institutions. All the well-known phrases of social gospel idealism are found in abundance here, as in most of Page's works—the family of God, brotherhood of man, a new social order, Kingdom of God on earth, the "mind of Jesus," divine love and goodwill, social justice, the way of the Cross, and the like.[2]

Page is possessed of a firm confidence in the intellectual, moral and spiritual capacities of human nature, as well as of a general optimism in regard to social change and institutional reconstruction. In his *Individualism and Socialism* (1933), he explains why Christianity so far has failed to produce a cooperative commonwealth, a Kingdom of God on earth. In his judgment the reasons are obvious: theology has been individualistic and personal, the historical insight of leaders inadequate, lack of training in economics prevalent among Christians, fellowship of religious leaders too intimate with the privileged, the church "entangled with capitalism," and clergy and laity too overwhelmed by vested interests (pp. 306–8). Yet he saw in this depression period a new day arising, indeed an imminent revolution in Christian social thought in America. "Accuracy demands that one hasten to say that organized religion is far less entangled with the prevailing economic system now than it was in 1929. It is not an exaggeration to say that *a revolution in thought on economic questions is occurring within the churches.*" *

* Note that Page puts in italics his judgment on the coming revolution. But he immediately adds—after rejoicing over the rapid increase in "out-and-out Socialists among ministers"—that only "a bare beginning has been made in

His latest works breathe the same hopeful spirit, despite an honest portrayal of ominous trends. In *The Will of God For These Days* (1945), the social evangelist declares that men can do the will of God in "economic life," can achieve what he describes as "mutuality." Government is good, is a means of developing such mutuality. In fact, public or "common" ownership *is a form of mutuality.** He says that we not only can prevent World War No. 3, but we could have prevented World War No. 2. And after presenting a terrifying description of the contemporaneous international situation, as well as a sordid "record of the churches" in supporting wars through the centuries, he prophesies in *Now is the Time to Prevent A Third World War* (1945), that "during the years immediately ahead we may expect the churches to dissociate themselves officially from the war system to an even more extreme degree. General conferences, general assemblies, national conventions will declare in more and more resolute tones that it is a sin to prepare to engage in the massacre of atomic war and that it is the will of God that Christians should run risks and take the consequences of resolutely following the Prince of Peace." †

Thus it is easy to see that Kirby Page is a true son of the social gospel tradition. Many of his literary efforts have been devoted to an account of the life, teachings and personality of Jesus. His supreme desire, his professed objective, has been an intensive, direct application of the love ethic to political, economic, racial and international problems. So far as the approach to institutional recon-

---

extricating organized religion from the embrace of capitalism." *Individualism and Socialism*, p. 309.

* The whole of Chapter VI titled "The Will of God in Economic Life" should be read, especially pp. 101, 103, 114 f. Here the author singles out the quest for "mutuality" as the doing of God's will. Subjectively mutuality seems to be the spirit of goodwill, cooperation, self-giving service. Objectively it is a society or an institution organized around the ideal of public welfare.

† P. 55 (Paper edition). Again he writes: "During the First World War there was only a tiny handful of Christian pacifist ministers in the United States. In a quarter-century this number has grown into a substantial minority. There is every indication that this growth will be still more rapid during the next decades." *The Will of God for These Days*, p. 161.

struction is concerned, his basic outlook is a combination of religious idealism, unqualified pacifism, and socialist politics. The church to him is one among the many agencies working for the Kingdom of God which must be established in this present world. In his opinion individuals, churches and nations must renounce categorically imperialism, nationalism, class hatred, race divisions, capitalistic profit-seeking, militarism and international war. And they can do so if they clearly understand the mind of Jesus in the light of the demands of their age and then set themselves resolutely to the task. In the face of the unprecedented imperative for a religious reconstruction of society, he releases a volume "upon the conviction that our problems could be solved if we could multiply sufficiently the number of men and women who are really Christian in enough areas of life." *

Let us now examine more closely the system of ideas which characterize the social thought of this religious revolutionary. In the first place he rejects capitalism uncompromisingly, whether viewed as a business pattern, a culture phenomenon or a system of moral and social values. In the early twenties it would appear that Page held the hope of Christianizing capitalism, that is, of infusing the economic order with the spirit of service and goodwill. In "The William Penn Lecture for 1922," delivered at Philadelphia,[3] the "desire to serve" is identified with the "motives of Jesus," the assumption being that economic arrangements need to be informed with a new set of motivations. "The self-denial and unselfish service of Jesus are not contrary to human nature," he maintains. What is needed is not a changed human nature, "but the creation of situations in which more social tendencies may more easily be given expression."[4] Industrial production must be for "social use," not "personal profit," and conducted not by "selfish competition" but by "friendly cooperation."

* The Will of God for These Days (Foreword). For an earlier statement of this hope see his article in Dynamic Faith (edited by David R. Porter, 1927), titled "The Christian View of Society." Here Page says: "The effort to build the family of God on earth offers the members of this generation the maximum opportunity for self-expression. . . . Let him who would probe most deeply into the meaning of life enroll in the ranks of those who have completely dedicated themselves to the task of building, here and now, the Divine Commonwealth" (pp. 43 f).

In 1922 he served as chairman for a committee which prepared a small volume titled *Christianity and Economic Problems*, released as A Discussion Group Textbook under the auspices of the Educational Committee of the Commission on the Church and Social Service of the Federal Council of Churches.[5] The book raises for consideration such questions as "Do Great Fortunes Help or Hinder Social Progress?" (Chapter IV), "What Degree of Public Control of Industry Will Best Promote the General Welfare?" (Chapter X) and "How Rapidly Can a Christian Economic Order Be Achieved?" (Chapter XI). The issues are presented in a strictly objective, noncommittal fashion, with a careful weighing of pros and cons, each chapter ending with questions for discussion. The conclusion is drawn that a new cooperative society can be established "during the twentieth century" as a result of "intimate acquaintance, a sharing of thought and experience, mutual outpouring and ingathering, a common search for truth, a mutual desire to serve, and cooperation in the common task of achieving a Christian economic order." [6] There is no hint that capitalism is an implacable foe of this projected democratic-Christian commonwealth and that it must be destroyed. Rather is there a general tone of optimism looking toward intelligent, orderly and peaceful change. Though the opening chapter is given the ominous title of "A Divided World," the claim is made that "conditions can be changed. These are days of transition. If only we have the intelligence and the will, a new and better day may be built." [7] Evidently Page assumes that the will, intelligence and enlightened self-interest of Christian statesmen and business men, along with the cooperation of a progressive church and organized labor, would be sufficient for a peaceful reorientation of capitalist industry and government toward the "Christian economic order."

But if during the decade following the First World War there existed any hope of converting capitalism by moral appeals, religious education, and arguments directed at the humanitarian sentiments or enlightened self-interest of business men, the depression was destined to shatter it completely.[8] By 1932–33 Page had become as uncompromisingly radical in regard to economic change as he was about the war-peace question. Henceforth he became an ardent socialist, as well as a pacifist and religious idealist. The volumes, *Living Crea-*

tively (1932), and *Individualism and Socialism* (1933), along with a series of editorials and articles between 1932 and 1934 (Cf. especially *The World Tomorrow*) are indicative of his political outlook. He rejects Communism or revolutionary Marxism on the one hand and capitalism or individualism, as he prefers to call it, on the other. The socialism which receives his enthusiastic support is of the parliamentary, evolutionary type such as is championed by the British Labour Party and the Socialist Party of America.

The invectives against the evils of capitalism are unsparing. "Poverty and strife are inherent in the present economic order," he charges. "Individual gain and competition are the corner-stones of capitalism." There are "five significant aspects of the struggle for private gain" resulting from competition: "planlessness, irresponsibility, inequity, consolidation and strife." [9] He quotes long passages from works like Arthur Pound's *The Iron Man,* Ward's *Which Way Religion?* and *Our Economic Morality,* and Stuart Chase's *The Nemesis of American Business* under general topics such as "Monotony," "The Perils of Inequality," "Mammon or God?," and "The Menace of Anarchy in Production." [10] The first four chapters of *Individualism and Socialism* are devoted in part to a sustained argument against the "theory of individualism" and in part to the cataloguing of a multitude of vicious practices and policies of which American business is guilty. After an analysis of socialist policy and strategy (Chapters V and VI), passages are then given over to a presentation of the "menace of fascism," to an exposure of the political conservatism of the Constitution and the Supreme Court, to an answer to popular prejudices against socialism, and to socialism's relation to religious idealism. He thus regards capitalism as a menace and a supreme challenge: "In this age men and women who refuse to uphold capitalism with all its brutality and exploitation will reproduce many of the experiences of the abolitionists who repudiated slavery. . . . And pacific revolution in America will not be wrought by men who are afraid of losing influence, position and income. Building a new world is a most perilous form of pioneering, and the most glorious victories of religion have ever been won in the hours of fiercest danger." [11]

Two pamphlets written probably about 1935, *Property* and *Capitalism and Its Rivals,* give some valuable materials regarding the political philosophy of this militant lay preacher. The latter is subtitled "A Comparative Interpretation of Individualism, New Dealism, Fascism, Communism, and Socialism." Page scores the "prevailing social system in the United States" which he says is "variously described as capitalism, individualism, and the profit system." This so-called free economy is operated according to the laissez-faire ideas and policies of men like Herbert Hoover and the spokesmen for the United States Chamber of Commerce. As for New Dealism, capitalism will be strengthened by it rather than weakened—contrary to opinions of witless business men and politicians who are terrified by its minimum controls. "The chief difference between Mr. Hoover and Mr. Roosevelt is found in *the degree of regulation of business by government* favored by these two statesmen." They do not "represent radically different schools of political thought. Both desire to strengthen and perpetuate capitalism." The New Deal is "not fascism or communism or socialism! Reformed individualism!" [12]

The interpretation of fascism is quite realistic, taking into consideration the complexity of the situations in Germany and Italy. Page avoids the too simple idea that fascism is a mere refuge of the wealthy classes, a clear-cut counter-revolution of the capitalists. Rather does he view it as a relatively unique but many-sided political phenomenon emerging from a fusion of racism, nationalism, political opportunism, the aftermath of war, and "the disintegration of capitalism." He is not inclined to blame too much the German political radicals who "failed to press forward and capture control of the government," for his assumption is that the hour of true revolution had not come. "Revolution cannot be achieved by will," he contends, although he admits that the blindness and opportunism of the Socialists contributed to their doom. Indeed, he is inclined to place even greater responsibility on the "blind and vindictive policy of the allies" which practically insured the wreckage of the Weimar Republic (See especially pp. 27-32). [13]

Communism of course is rejected in favor of a "pacific revolution" and of parliamentary, gradualistic collectivism. Opposition is given to communism because of its advocacy of violent class war, its belief in the necessity for proletarian dictatorship, its willingness to suppress civil liberties, and its dogmatic notion about the possibility of revolution in all countries. Page lays down the proposition that the Red Revolution in Russia was due to a remarkable and an unexpected concatenation of events, which is not likely to occur again. "The attempt to establish a just society in the United States through civil war against the owning class," he warns, "would almost certainly result in appalling misery and indescribable chaos." Not only must the orthodox Marxist objectives be renounced, but a united front of socialists, pacifists and liberals with the Communists as well. An effort at a united front would be a "terrible handicap rather than a strong asset." Socialists in refusing to lock arms with the Reds, even against fascism, are not possessed of cowardice but of "sound judgment." America needs a program of socialism well adapted to her peculiar conditions and controlled by ideals of peace, justice and democracy. In the section on "Socialism" the author makes reference to his *Individualism and Socialism* and to the pamphlet on *Property* for further details concerning his "program" for a new socialized American economy.

Aside from the aforementioned volume published in 1933 and the pamphlet, *Capitalism and Its Rivals,* the plea for pacifist socialism may be followed in *Property* (1935?) and in articles in *The World Tomorrow* for September 14, 1932, April 5, May, and October 26, 1933, and in the issue of June 14, 1934.[14] In the argument on "Property" the author contends that the crisis of modern life to a great extent is due to a serious maldistribution of property. The very concepts of property are outdated, as one can see from the nature of the modern corporation and its intolerable abuses. Aside from the horrors of poverty, irresponsible luxury, and class antagonisms, there is the ever-increasing menace of inefficiency. Such inefficiency is not a narrow technological matter—for there is undoubtedly a "high degree of industrial efficiency"—but an over-all wastefulness and lack of "correlation." The profit motive leads to restricted output, as unbiased research has proved beyond question! We need above all a wider distribution of "private property" in consumers' goods and a drastic curtailment of "private property" in the basic resources and industries. Planning of a socialist type can make this possible—and only such planning!

The viewpoint in the analysis is an unqualified socialism. Page

[78]

scores proposals for business "self-regulation," accepting the position that periodic depression is inherent in capitalism. He holds the socialist doctrine of the economic basis of political power. *"Government is dominated by the groups who wield the most powerful kind of power,* and in an industrial society that power is found in the control of the chief instruments of production and distribution" (*Ibid.,* p. 17). The system of taxation is inadequate, but can never be made adequate under a capitalist economy.[15] The benefits of a socialized order are as follows: balance between national saving and national spending, increased industrial productivity, reduction of unemployment, higher wages and salaries, and greater general efficiency.* In brief, "the program that I have outlined herein is," he acknowledges, "that of the Socialist Party of America, although not all Socialists will agree with everything that I have written." [16]

His article in *The World Tomorrow* under the title of "A Socialist Program of Deliverance" is a constructive statement of the broad outlines of the Socialist position in America, at least of its position during the thirties. Page here speaks of *"rapidly progressive non-warlike revolution,"* of avoiding "the illusion of utopia-via-violent-cataclysmic-revolution," and of "stepping forward vigorously along the pathway of socialist policies." He says in italics: "Rapid movement toward equality is conditioned upon the progressive transfer from private control to social ownership of the major means of production and distribution." [17] Four reasons are given as to why socialization is imperative: to eliminate the possibility of exploitation of the poor by the rich, to increase productivity (which increase socialization will make possible), to eliminate unemployment, and finally to make effective genuine social planning. The method for the achievement of a socialized America will be gradual and democratic, though with complete abolition of private ownership in the "chief instruments of production and distribution" at the "earliest possible moment." The actual process of transfer of ownership and control to public authority will begin with the banking and credit mechanism and certain all-important natural resources like coal, oil, and water power.

* One specific proposal is that incomes, *"so long as the minimum wage is not higher than $2,000,"* should be sharply limited to about $10,000, or even to $5,000. *Ibid.,* p. 31.

And the policy, most emphatically, is not to be by ruthless confiscation but by purchase, though heavy taxation is expected to absorb most of the liquid wealth passing into the hands of the dispossessed financial and industrial aristocrats.

Page faces frankly the gloomy but incontestable truth that full socialism is likely to come only by a capitalist collapse. He writes in italics: "Without doubt the primary factor in advancing these policies will be the breakdown or disintegration of capitalist efficiency." As for the agencies by which the program must triumph, we are to rely upon a triple organization: a solidified labor unionism, a consumers' co-operative movement and "voters in a Socialist Party." * For the "strategy of liberal Democrat-Republicans" which seeks "social control" not "consciously directed toward equality of economic privilege" and toward "public ownership" will more "firmly entrench vested interests." †

The author then offers a fifteen-point program for the establishment of a socialist democracy in the United States:

1. Government unemployment relief.
2. Federal subsidies to farmers.
3. "Drastic scaling down of debts."
4. Tax reductions on small properties and small incomes.
5. A bond issue of billions to provide work relief.
6. Social insurance reserves which are "more essential" than the "payment of dividends and interest in slack times."
7. "Minimum wage and the family wage."
8. Complete "abolition of child labor by state and federal statutes."
9. Reduction of working hours with maintenance of wage levels.
10. Extension of "free public privileges" like free education, art, music, recreation, health.
11. Progressive heavy taxation.
12. Rigorous control over public utilities and corporations.
13. Defense of civil liberties.
14. Withdrawal of positive financial and military support (by the federal Government) of industrial and finance capitalism.

* But acknowledgment is made that consumers' organization perhaps "is destined to play a minor role."

† He replies to a question put by Harry F. Ward as to what should be socialist tactics in case of critical class conflict by saying that three alternatives presented themselves: passivity, armed resistance to reaction, and "non-warlike resistance." Page urges adoption of the third alternative.

15. Total dissolution "of armed forces maintained for action against other nations."

Despite this advocacy of a radical reconstruction of the social order, involving a categorical repudiation of the capitalist system, both as a complex of cultural values and as an institutional framework, Page has a strong distaste for orthodox Marxism. He minces no words in denouncing the revolutionary tactics and utopian expectations of the Communist Party, as well as any suggestion of a united front movement. One of his articles is deliberately titled "Socialism Versus Communism" in which he argues that Socialists believe in class consciousness but not in "class hatred and class warfare" like the Communists. He opposes any political program or organization which would "utilize the military method in seeking to create the classless society." Socialists, he insists, believe that the reckless strategy of the Reds is "entirely fallacious and highly dangerous" in the United States. Moreover, the idea that American capitalism is in "dying convulsions is nonsense," and attempts at proletarian revolution of the Marxist brand "would instantly drive America into the arms of fascism." The Communist doctrine of violent class war is regarded as "highly unethical and unjustfiable"; and hence he renounces such a philosophy and strategy "on pragmatic grounds as well as from ethical considerations."

Again, the contention is laid down that pacifist revolution is realistic while violent revolution is fanciful and sentimental. He feels that though "successful revolution" may not come to pass "for this generation of Americans," nonetheless "it is more romantic to anticipate the creation of a Socialist commonwealth in the United States by means of civil war than it is to put faith in a non-military combination of political action and economic pressure through a triple organization of workers, consumers and voters. Not the pacifist revolutionist, but the violent revolutionist is the sentimentalist." [18] In 1932 he wrote also that "it is far easier and more desirable to persuade America to adopt the Socialist program than it is to attempt revolution by violence." [19] Hence he declared himself in favor of a recent manifesto —this was during the depression—issued by the British Labour Party, the Parliamentary Labour Party, and the British Trades Union Congress. The manifesto clung to the faith in the "broadest democratic principles" and in a "united working-class movement" acting on these principles. Likewise, concludes Page, we in America "cannot at the same time seek a democratic state and a dictatorship. We cannot follow both a pacifist procedure and a militarist method." *

An essential element in this position is pacifism both as a religio-ethical standard and as a political technique. The crusader never fails to make emphatic the religious basis of his rejection of violence. He insists on following the so-called method of Jesus: "Jesus refuses to accept the status quo, with all its injustice and misery. He refrains from hatred and violence, but attacks entrenched iniquity with the utmost vigor and abandon." [20] Page feels compelled to avoid any violence which is a "violation of the family spirit," which is not "restraining and redemptive." [21] Again, "every person is a child of God and a brother of man. Therefore personality is the supreme value, and should be regarded as an end and not merely as a means to an end. Brother should act toward brother in ways that are consistent with brotherhood. If coercion of every kind is an inherent denial of the family spirit, then it is immoral." [22]

Yet in his opinion it is possible to utilize non-violent methods of coercion which render such pressures ethical, "restraining and redemptive." Repudiating a technique of mere moral suasion, he admits that "persuasion by itself will not suffice; but fortunately ethical forms of coercion are available." He does not hesitate to assert that "there is only a remote possibility of converting enough property owners to make possible the transformation of the present economic order by voluntary action from the top." "That the millions of miserable victims of capitalism will wait for this age-long process to alleviate their suffering appears wholly unlikely." [23] In an article on "The Future of the Fellowship" [24] he said that there were three methods urged by various members of the F.O.R. (all radicals nonetheless): (1) The method of moral suasion, education, self-sacrifice,

* From the article in *The World Tomorrow,* May, 1933, titled "Can Socialists and Communists Unite?" p. 396. Another main reason for opposing united front plans is that efforts at close cooperation with Communists always resulted in unfair tactics on the part of the latter who are by doctrine and practical policy committed to a ruthless destruction of all Socialist or so-called "social-fascist" parties.

but involving renunciation of *all forms of coercion* (italics mine), (2) The method of "economic and political coercion" short of "armed violence," (3) The method of armed violence when it becomes a bitter necessity for workers. Page identifies himself with the second technique (2), but further qualifies his position by refusing to abandon the workers if conflict should drive them to violence. He would serve workers during class war (or serve their families) in various ways, but not "sanction the use of armed force." [25]

It is clear, therefore, that this rebel against the status quo regards non-violent force as an effective political expedient. In 1932, while urging action against Japanese aggression in China, he argues that "moral condemnation, diplomatic boycott, and an embargo against Japanese silk" offer an alternative to inaction on the one hand and "violent hostilities" on the other. And this gets results, with "less suffering and more possibilities of a pacific settlement." [26] In an article written in reply to an editorial in *The Christian Century*, Page branded as unjustified the assumption that recent discussion and argument by F.O.R. members over pacifist principles was "wholly hypothetical" and "unrealistic." [27] He retorted that the vast majority of the Fellowship of Reconciliation were opposed to all industrial "war" as "distinguished from 'struggle' in which various types of non-military and non-warlike coercion are used." He adds that rejection of violence or "warlike" methods does not mean neutrality in the "struggle between the classes." [28]

Pacifism as a political strategy is strongly advocated in international affairs. Here Page has rendered a unique service in assembling and publishing an enormous volume of facts about the problem of war and peace.[29] An article titled "If War is to Be Abolished" (1934) gives a digest of his essential position. He recommends five steps as a "program of action" for the establishment of permanent peace.[30] First, we must "abolish the system of private property in the chief means of production and distribution." Secondly, there must be an "unequivocal repudiation" of "armed intervention" designed to protect American property and life in foreign lands. Thirdly, absolute disarmament, for our danger lies not in the "vicious aggressiveness" of a potential enemy but in "an international system of economics and politics which produces catastrophic explosions."

Fourthly, a building of strong "international agencies of justice" is imperative. And finally there must be "war resistance," both individually and in mass movements. In regard to the fifth point we are urged to membership in The Fellowship of Reconciliation and in the War Resisters' League, as well as to work for a general unification of all pacifists into "a powerful war resisters' movement."

In his recent book, *Now Is the Time to Prevent a Third World War,* the fundamental approach is unaltered. We are given here a vivid description of the horrors of atomic war, with a reassertion of the pacifist principle that war is "a combination of all the worst evils which threaten the human race" and hence that there is no possibility of selecting a "lesser evil." The author contends that feverish military preparation actually increases the danger of conflict and makes impossible "mutual understanding and mutual confidence." He urges us to an understanding of the "dynamics of Soviet foreign policy," to an attempt to sense the socio-psychological roots of Russia's dogmas about capitalism, war, and proletarian dictatorship, as well as to consideration of the basis of her suspicion of the United Nations organization.* He contends that there is no real security in any "armed security," and thus discounts the Security Council of the U.N. in favor of the General Assembly. The recommendation is for "mutual aid" as an alternative to a police force. "The hope," he avers, "is not in collective military coercion. That road leads straight to the abyss." The way out lies in the "utilization of the facilities of the Economic and Social Council, the Assembly, the Security Council, the International Court of Justice, the International Labor Organization, and other agencies of international government." [31] As for America's domestic problem: "The Socialist Party should become the nucleus of a new political party supported by organized labor, organized farmers, organized consumers, as has long been maintained by Norman Thomas and other Socialists." [32]

* In our judgment Page's analysis includes as fair, balanced and realistic an understanding of Russia as can be found in contemporary American political thought. Indeed, his is one of those rare reactions to Sovietism in which an underlying element of fear and aversion (or of contempt) is not evident. The statement is all the more remarkable as it was uttered at the time of a rising tide of anti-Russian hysteria which tended to help make the international scene such a tangled and tragic spectacle.

For a final glimpse at Page's Christian-pacifist socialism let us note certain aspects of the argument in *The Will of God for These Days* (1945). He urges the Christian church, which he designates as a "holy fellowship," to a "total allegiance to Jesus Christ," that is, to be "totally surrendered to Jesus Christ as Lord." This means "commitment to his way of life," following him "in race relations, economic life and international affairs." The basic religious attitude is love, with all men viewed as God's creatures. As a Christian approach to economic behavior we must have an attitude of humble interdependence, of gratitude and unworthiness, of the renunciation of greed, self-interest, self-centeredness. We must avoid "pagan" incentives, realizing that the Christian virtues are "adequate incentives to efficient and sustained economic activity." (pp. 79–82). A repetition is made of the fact that high wages and wide consumption are more important than "interest and dividends" (p. 85). He calls attention to a trend toward common ownership, even in the collectivist character of corporate business (p. 94). Real laissez faire has been abandoned long ago anyway, he declares, for the government has always fought on the side of business and investors (p. 102). The demand today is for free highways, bridges, education, public recreation, hospitals, socialized medicine, and various types of common ownership, particularly for cooperatives and "common ownership by citizens of municipalities and counties and states and the nations" (p. 93).

It is noteworthy, however, that the word "socialism" has dropped out, being replaced by "mutuality." Public or common ownership is declared to be a form of mutuality; and government itself is an agency for mutuality or public welfare.* The TVA is an instance of a program of "mutuality," as is any extension of social ownership by democratic means. Obviously the "will of God" for us is that we work to create a socialized economy, that we seek to achieve mutuality now on a small scale, even in desultory fashion. The as-

* Page here looks upon government not as an evil nor as an agent of oppression à la Marxism, but as an agent of social good, that is, as an instrument of social welfare (or "mutuality," as he now calls it). Throughout his previous works he is torn between a welfare concept and a Marxist concept, as is true of most of the theological radicals discussed in these pages.

sumption is that the quest for a socialist order—that is, an order of "mutuality"—is the political expression of the Christian's obedience to the will of God. Presumably also those resisting socialization are trying to oppose the divine imperative, though perhaps ignorantly. A socialist philosophy is for him the proper Christian political ideal in America. Moreover, he appears to have no fear of the reputed evil consequences of socialization, particularly of the dangers of dictatorship often said to be inherent in the extension of large-scale governmental power over the economy.*

As for international policy, Page argues that it is contrary to God's will when we, the nation, go to war. He believes that "peace now" (in 1945 with the war in progress) is preferable to victory. God is absolutely an anti-war God just as Jesus was anti-war, or at least "holy and righteous in all his ways." Thus it is taken for granted that God has a purpose for the nation, which purpose the nation renounces when it goes to war. Page insists that as a follower of Christ he cannot go with the majority who want war, but only with the minority who are determined to do God's will regardless of cost or consequences. Though he seems to acknowledge (rather casually) that our civilization may be doomed, Christians can build a Kingdom "within our hearts and in all human relationships" (pp. 162 f.).

It is rather difficult to do full justice to the many aspects and details of Kirby Page's social thought. It is only fair to acknowledge that here is a man with a *feel for the facts,* that here is one who possesses a remarkable passion for coming to grips concretely with political and economic problems. Nonetheless he remains an idealist of the type which never quite escapes the temptation to indulge in some rather treacherous prophecies. While giving a gloomy picture of the paralyzing worldliness of the church, he sees a great awakening involving a widespread understanding of Jesus' demands on society. After building a case for the power of Christian devotion only to save a "faithful remnant," he then falls back on preaching rather

* On pp. 156 f. he takes another fling at capitalism, charging American culture with being degrading and disintegrating. Indeed, contemporary civilization is experiencing "a cumulative harvest of disintegration, decay, conflict, destruction, desolation" (pp. 153 f.). Again, he uses not the word "capitalism" but "individualism."

[86]

than on the ruthless logic of the somber facts he presents.[33] What he actually demonstrates is not the ability of Christian love to "save" civilization, but merely the moral grandeur of faithfulness to an absolute ideal.

Indeed Page occasionally gets himself into some rather embarrassing inconsistencies. He presents overwhelming evidence of the disintegration of Christian-capitalist culture and then argues that "the gospel of Jesus is now more clearly understood and followed with more fidelity by a larger minority than ever before." Is it really true, let us ask, that Jesus Christ is being followed more faithfully by professed Christians than ever before, and indeed by those immersed in the values of a decadent culture? How can Page call people members of God's faithful remnant who in their corporate life willingly and often boastfully do all the evil things which he has just described in this volume as contrary to God's will? Chapter IV on "total allegiance to Jesus Christ" apparently was written to show that only those who carry out God's will in economic, political and racial affairs are the true Christians. But he ends by declaring that a Christian may belong to the "faithful company" and yet in "some of his relationships be far removed from the inner circle." Thus at a stroke he throws all the worldly Christians out of the Kingdom at the front door and then brings them back through the window.

It is perhaps not best here to enter into any argument concerning his pacifism which is both a religious ideal and a political strategy. The debate on this question is interminable and would require many pages just to state various aspects of the issue. Suffice it to say that he usually judges the Christian value or unchristian evil of an act of coercion in terms of its objective effects rather than in terms of motive as Jesus appears to have done. He almost invariably illustrates the problem and the solution of political, economic or international questions by some homely example of personal or family relations as if a simple application of the "family pattern" to all social problems would take care of the matter. There is the further presumption that if coercion is non-violent it has a good chance to "ennoble personality."

His optimism and idealism is revealed in his too simple faith in "pacific revolution," which confidence is based upon the belief that men even in their collective capacities are moved mainly by high moral and rational considerations. In thinking of a reconstructed America he describes how easy it would be to socialize industry upon the decay of capitalism. Only the financial and industrial interests will stand in the way of the coming people's revolution!—as if this were a molehill and not a mountain! [34] He seems to overlook the momentous fact that in carrying out the schemes suggested by him the presumption is that the masses have already been converted unequivocally to the *idea* of a socialized economy. His description is all very beautiful; and it seems so obvious, clear-cut and rational that he actually predicts a new political alignment in six years (1935–1941?).[35] But—and here is the rub!—our whole culture is dominated by the capitalist ethos, by an irrational sentiment toward individualistic "democracy," "free enterprise," the virtue of property and profits, with very few people really committed to this *new order*. The menace of totalitarianism and of communism tends to inspire the opponents of fundamental change with prophetic zeal in defense of the status quo. Most Americans are not enthusiastic even about a mild, non-violent, gradualistic movement like consumer cooperation. There is certainly little evidence of a great coming national movement championing socialism.

Our final illustration of Page's social gospel faith is found in his demand for pacific revolution in world affairs. His repudiation of coercion is so extreme that he frowns upon the idea of an international police force. In fact his fundamental argument, as seen in Chapter I of his *Now Is the Time to Prevent a Third World War*, is somewhat question-begging. For he would eliminate international explosions by utilizing values and structures which themselves if not utterly impossible are at least as difficult to achieve as is the abolition of atomic war. The matter of the prevention of war through "mutual aid," through "international law," "agencies of world government," and "mutual confidence" *constitutes the problem*. This is the other side of the war-peace problem, and hence Page's "solution" is a mere tautology.

6

Christian Marxism:
Harry F. Ward

FOR A GENERATION Harry F. Ward has held a commanding place
in the religious social thought of the nation. He was a younger
contemporary of Walter Rauschenbusch, in 1912 editing the *Social
Creed of the Churches* and in 1914 the *Year Book of the Church and
Social Service in the United States*. At the end of the First World
War he was quickly recognized as a foremost spokesman for applied Christianity, by speech, writing and political agitation demonstrating his unusual power as a social critic.

Since those early days respect for his ability has grown by leaps
and bounds, pushing him into various strategic positions. He has
been secretary of the Methodist Federation for Social Service, and
chairman of the American Civil Liberties Union, as well as of the
American League Against War and Fascism. Numerous journals
have sought for his contributions. For twenty-three years (1918–
1941), he occupied the chair of Professor of Christian Ethics at the
Union Theological Seminary, New York, in which position by
means of lectures, books, pamphlets and social action he exercised
far-reaching influence over political and economic thinking inside
and outside the theological world.

Among the social thinkers dealt with here Ward is one of the less
difficult to describe because, though his ideas since the Great War
of 1914–18 have taken on an arresting change (at least in emphasis),

[89]

here is a remarkable coherence in most of his analyses and theories. Despite an occasional jibe at the "social gospel," he is one of the best examples of such a gospel as we have defined it in these pages. To him religion is mainly a moral force to be used as an instrument to rebuild society. The theological question is a secondary matter. God is known through "ethical action," he proclaims, and religion today must set itself up as demanding "a new order of life" or it will become "court chaplain" to the status quo. What we need is not a restoration of "intellectual or esthetic religion," as in the "new orthodoxy," but a socialized faith united intimately with ethics and sociology as the keys to the "new order." [1] Conjoined with this "ethical" Christianity is a politics which moved in the fifteen years between 1918 and 1933 from a pronounced anti-capitalist, democratic utopianism to a virtually unqualified religious socialism of the most radical type. At the close of the first European conflict Ward was an aggressive democratic idealist thoroughly disgusted with the capitalist ethos and demanding numerous reforms. By the middle of the depression he was an unapologetic Marxist with an intense admiration for Sovietism, although the hope of modifying Marxism by Christian ethics and democratic principles was never abandoned. Perhaps the best clue to his most mature thinking in its various facets is found in *Democracy and Social Change*, 1940.

1. Ward's Early Christian-Democratic Utopianism

With the return of peace in Europe men saw not only numerous stirrings throughout the colonial world but the birth of the League of Nations and the explosion of the Russian Revolution. These postwar years with their apparent foreshadowing of a new era found Ward in the vanguard of the social gospel movement. *The New Social Order* written by him in 1919 contains all the fundamental doctrines and perspectives of the prevailing American social Christianity. The title of the volume is itself not without significance. Here was an utterance which not only prophesied the dawning of a glorious new world, but which boldly set forth the "principles and programs" destined to create it. The author affirmed that this book contained "certain principles or ideals" which "are now being consciously accepted by multitudes of people as the guiding stars of life and the working principles of a new social order." [2] The achievement of such a democratic Christian utopia was to be "a task for religion as well as for economic and social science and practical organization."

An examination of the contents of *The New Social Order* brings into clear light the mental outlook, the political philosophy, the ethical and religious assumptions, the procedures and strategies of what was then regarded as the most progressive Christianity. In the first place, capitalist society was under bombardment for its selfishness, competitiveness, materialism, inequality, autocracy. "The masters of economic power in our modern civilization," he accuses, "have really a greater dominion over men than was achieved by the emperors of old." They can by "decisions concerning the prices of products, the wages, and indeed the whole terms and course of industry" not simply "take toll and tribute from the productive labor of a nation or of several nations" but even determine the whole course of life and opportunity (p. 67). As the warrior was the aristocratic justification for the ruling classes of the past, so is the "pioneer captain of industry and finance for the ruling classes of an industrial civilization" (p. 79). As for America, the "country which prides itself on being the great example and exponent of democracy is in its industrial life the most autocratic of all the great industrial nations" (p. 67). Here is the "central struggle of the modern democratic movement . . . the struggle for the control of the means of life, of the resources of the earth and of labor power" (p. 64). The need of mankind is not for just a "reconstruction" but a radically "new social order." "What is going on," Ward explains with touching ardor, "is no mere tinkering with the machinery of human society but one of those tremendous upheavals which mark a new period in human living" (p. 8). Business in the United States does not want a new world; it has no "understanding of the perilous condition in which the present political and economic order both stand, or of the determination of the common people the world over to change not only their social condition but also the causes that have led to the condition" (p. 324). The "rulers of the democratic capitalistic state" are morally and spiritually of the "same caliber as the ruling class of imperialistic militarism, and bear a similar relationship to the future welfare of the common folk" (p. 363). But mankind is on the march and cannot be stopped!

Chapter XII, the final one, is a fitting climax to this dream of a democratic utopia. It is appropriately titled "The Trend of Progress." A new world of brotherhood is breaking out everywhere. Progress is inherent in the universe, though temporarily the stream sometimes "eddies and its main currents turn upon themselves." People are generally growing wiser, having been "rapidly educated in the last five years to an understanding of the necessity of applying these principles if the race is to live in the future" (pp. 356 f.). The Great War heightened mankind's vision of this need, for one of the "strangest phenomena of the war" was the tremendous growth in cooperatives "in every country where they were in existence." "The capitalist order is passing, not because of defects in its machinery, but because its power is giving out" (p. 368). Indeed, the well-known "Social Creed of the Churches" contains the principles which "if followed to their conclusion would result in a new social order" (p. 329).

Even these numerous quotations from Ward's lyric to progress and to a coming universal enlightenment do not portray adequately the scope and depth of such social gospel faith. Only the actual reading of the text can convey a truly vivid impression of this almost mystical, Condorcet-like optimism. After a general introductory chapter there are set forth the "principles of the new order"—listed as equality, universal service, efficiency, the supremacy of personality, and solidarity. All of these ideals or "principles" are expounded in detail in five successive chapters. Equality is declared to be one part of the "charter of democracy" and universal service the other part. In the discussion of "social efficiency" we are told that the new order must rest on science, that modern chaos is due to uncoordinated ideals and knowledge, that our need is agreement on common purposes in education, religion, industry and government, that greed and graft may be overcome by scientific ideas and instruments. The achievement of "social efficiency" has as its end a vastly greater productivity, distribution and consumption. But, asks the expositor, if we strive for maximum productivity, for wealth, goods, great social organization—to what end is all this? He then gives the answer. Here is the chief end of it all—"the supremacy of personality"! At this point the argument approaches an attitude which reveals a mind overwhelmed by confidence in man's conquest of the world: "In the past many generations of men have worked in the dark like coral insects, living and dying without any conscious choice concerning ends, not knowing what life meant except to eat and drink and beget and fight and die. But now we build in the light. We have learned what these folks of the past were doing and how they did it" (p. 133). Knowing the riddle of the universe, knowing its purpose as the creation of autonomous, free personality, man "can defy the world," and "with his body smashed to fragments [can] go out into the future in a supreme assertion of himself" (p. 137).

The picture given in the volume is not complete without Part II with its description of "programs for the new order." Here Ward sees in the British Labour Party, the Soviet System, the League of Nations and in certain American movements the death of capitalist industrialism.* He interprets the upheaval of World War No. 1, as well as the rise of labor and socialistic schemes, as signs of the times. He is convinced of the possibility of the orderly direction of change; and hence for him the building of a "new order" is about like the construction of a huge house. Indeed, he actually uses the figure, giving "Four Pillars of the House" which would rest upon the "democratic control of society in all its activities."

Two other literary products of the period illustrate fully the same general viewpoint. One is *The Gospel for a Working World,* and the other is *The Opportunity for Religion.*[3] The former book, avowedly dealing with the basic problem of labor and industry, appeals to the church to Christianize all of life, especially economic institutions, organizations, processes and relations. It displays a

* In the United States the prophetic movements were the Socialist Party, various Independent Labor parties, the farmers' Non-Partisan League (promoting "state socialism" in 1918), the National Women's Trade Union League of America, and "some Reconstruction Programs" of business during the War. He is quite skeptical of the value of the last-mentioned, however, as must be admitted. Nor does he have confidence in the possibilities of the American Federation of Labor, for its leadership is "not the voice of the rank and file."

religious-democratic utopianism in its total outlook, although one must acknowledge that the contents reveal a remarkable concentration on the knotty details of wages, hours, standards of living, child labor, work conditions, wealth distribution, trade unionism and the like. Speaking of Christianity's great opportunity of the present hour, Ward declares that "the final test of all religions is in the field of social action." [4] Society today possesses "large religious forces" some of which are "particularly to be found in the world of labor." As for the prospects of mankind: "The laws of the physical universe, the history of the human race, the causes of social progress and decay—these are all an open book before this generation. The control of nature and of human society is now in the hand of the common people to an extent unimagined by even the leaders of the past. Not blindly as did men of other days do we take the road. We are not walking in darkness." [5]

All through the twenties Ward maintained a keen interest in economic and political reforms. He was especially concerned about the status of organized labor, and wrote voluminously on its behalf.[6] During this time there was hardly a greater champion of civil liberties in the country. Political upheavals anywhere in the world struck a responsive chord in him. He published articles about the Chinese situation, about India's struggles, about Sovietism. His strictures on capitalism—on its immorality, its money-mindedness, its ruthless competition, its anti-labor tactics, its tendency toward autocracy—continued to mount in intensity. Perhaps his greatest obsession was the utterly un-Christian nature of the so-called profit motive which he unceasingly declared to be irreconcilable with the ethical teaching of Jesus.[7] He always saw an absolute conflict between the "two gospels," that is, the "gospel of Mammon and the gospel of God" preached by Jesus and demanded of true Christians. One is the service motive, the other the profit motive! In an article in *The Christian Century* (December 27, 1923), he argued that if the "law of profit" is scientifically true, "then is our preaching vain, and our faith is also vain, insofar as the development of the Kingdom of God in the earth is concerned."

In 1928–29, just before the depression, his fury against capitalist culture became unbounded. It was then that he wrote *Our Economic*

Morality and the Ethic of Jesus, a book which even today impresses one as an almost unrivalled indictment of America's social morality so far as contemporary religious literature is concerned. And the volume is not without keen analyses of economic institutions and processes. At the particular moment, however, the anti-capitalist attitude of this radical teacher of Christian ethics had not driven him to embrace Marxism; but the next few years reveal a positive movement in that direction.

Let us look more closely at the nature of the argument contained in *Our Economic Morality.* He begins by ruling out of economics the possibility of strict objectivity, declaring that "the issue between the critics and the protagonists of competitive profit seeking is not to be decided by evidence alone." It is also a matter of value judgment and of sentiment! He chides the conservative economists for their pseudo-objectivity. They argue "as though no sentiment attached to the defense of orthodox economics and the maintenance of the status quo! As though sentiments are not also facts! As though there could be any social science that did not deal with the whole of man's life!" [8] Hence there can be no separation of morality and economics, no ignoring of the ultimate economic consequences of ethical principles.

In the opening chapters Ward lays down the contention that capitalist morality is completely alien to the Christian ideal, is economically unworkable, and indeed is based on an outmoded "sterile philosophy." He maintains that the essential historic Christian ethic —an ethic of solidarity, cooperation, mutual aid—is diametrically opposed to the basic social ethics of American industrial civilization. The profit-seeking, competitive spirit of the prevailing order, its acquisitive "economic morality," is the main challenge to Christianity which is expressed in the "ethic of Jesus." "If this philosophy works, then obviously the ethic of Jesus will not work; for they are opposites" (p. 46). Capitalism is accused of stopping progress, but by this is meant spiritual or moral progress with which is identified the extension of equalitarian and democratic ideas and institutions. The Kingdom of God, "an organized commonwealth," leads in the "opposite direction from the industrialist philosophy of the beneficence of self-interest, the automatic operation of greed for the common good" (pp. 47 f.).* Capitalism offers no future for the human race! It is now disintegrating; for the "signs multiply that the times are ripe and rotten ripe for a change" (p. 286).†

Yet man holds his destiny in his hands. He is not bound by rigid economic or natural forces. Here the rebel attacks economic determinism in both its capitalist and Marxist versions. "It is time for the idea of the infallibility of self-interest—in its Socialist as well as the Capitalistic form—to go to the museum with the other infallibilities" (p. 292). Though Communism is a challenge to Christianity, though its "doctrine of economic determinism" is like a "type of evangelical religion," it nevertheless offers a dangerous principle. All types of fatalistic, deterministic views must be abandoned. "The Calvinist relies upon an over-ruling providence, the Catholic upon Holy Church, the Communist upon economic predestinarianism; he literally finds God in the machine" (p. 295). The capitalist philosophy, of course, since it holds the "hypothesis that human nature is mostly swinish," is thus a creed of "economic fundamentalists" (p. 65).

But ethical religion can point the way out. The ethic of Jesus is revolutionary, asking "man to create the future not merely to obey what went before." Jesus "bade men seek that justice and fellowship which was historically crystallized in the phrase, the Kingdom of God." However, we must reject the prevailing morality of industrialism and embrace its opposite—"the elements conserved and developed by the ethic of Jesus and upon which it relies for the future

---

* The assumption is made, however, that capitalists and their supporters consciously reject the Christian ethic (p. 19). They do not as a rule. On the contrary they tend to identify their codes, aspirations and "principles" with the so-called Christian ideals of work, thrift, devotion to business obligation, ambition, charitableness, democratic sentiment. Ward later acknowledges this fact in his analysis of the "economic virtues." (pp. 238 ff.)

† Interestingly enough, while Ward talks frequently of "social efficiency," and while several times he refers to Veblen and Stuart Chase, he never quite strikes directly the now familiar *economic* indictment of capitalism. His perspective is invariably a moral one. On p. 26, for instance, he refers to Veblen's distinction between capitalist "business" and capitalist technology. This only shows Ward that technological advance, co-operative plant management and engineering are examples of a demand for a *co-operative* order!

of man—the supremacy of personality, the obligation of service, the need of solidarity, the validity of sacrifice" (pp. 287, 305, 311). Protestantism must shake off its past connections with aristocratic Puritan ideals and become a new revolutionary religion. Jesus' principle is a well-balanced social ethic superior to all the contending economic moralities of the day. "For what shall man live? For all, says Communism. For each, says Individualism. For both, says the ethic of Jesus" (p. 319). He scores "class-limited churches in both suburb and slum," as well as the "fundamentalist" spokesmen for the Crisis Theology, who to him are endeavoring, like Pharisees, "to use both worlds for their own self-interest." He brands the new European supernaturalism as a "purely theological religion" deeply influenced by capitalism.*

Our Economic Morality is full of flashes of insight too numerous to discuss here. Ward points out the demand for economic equality as a basis for the future extension of democracy. He exposes the hypocritical use by conservatives of the idea of "inexorable economic law," as well as the habit of business in manipulating the so-called automatic market to its advantage against the consumer. There is a hint at the discrepancy between economic thinking and economic trends, "our prevailing economic philosophy" no longer being "even a description, let alone an explanation, of the facts." The question is raised of the ultimate issue of capitalism turning around the matter of its efficiency, the presumption being that a system that does not work satisfactorily cannot endure indefinitely regardless of the desperation of its defenders. In attacking Bukharin's materialism he also rejects his oversimplified theory of social causation, for, as Ward says, "neither spiritual life nor material production is cause alone; each operates constantly as both cause and effect." Again, with real insight he points out the essentially futile efforts of piecemeal planning, or as he puts it, "co-operation for profit." He argues that in a

* The appeal to American Protestantism is apparently to a rather vague, disembodied religion which evidently is not, as he elsewhere says, "the religion of the middle class." Or perhaps he expects the middle-class Protestants to shake off their bourgeois mentality and morality. At least this is the logic of the appeal.

profit system these little pockets of co-operation ultimately intensify competition.*

Yet in this volume Ward remains the democratic-Christian utopian with absolute confidence in science, sociology and the inherent wisdom of the common man. The demand of religion is "to spiritualize all of life by setting man to work to realize the best that he has dared to dream." Christian ethics can supply a new moral ideal for society so that in "any society peaceful evolution is possible" as an alternative to revolutionary change. He formulates the basic question so as to place mankind at the crossroads: "Either religion proves itself able to bring the acquisitive society redemption from the making and selling of things, and release from the struggle of greed for power, or it blindly leads this blind age into the twilight that has fallen upon all other civilizations" (pp. 322 f.). And his faith in human nature and the law of progress inclines him in regard to the issue to believe in the triumph of reason, faith, justice and the milk of human kindness. Civilization can be saved from catastrophe!

In his next major work, *Which Way Religion?* (1931), which is described by the author as a "tract for the times," Ward's essential outlook is unchanged. The initial chapter, titled "The Choice Before Us"—that is, the choice before the organized religious forces and institutions—is a broadside against many trends regarded as unhealthy. Warning is given about the encroachment of state power on religious liberty, the temptation of the church to glorify war, the political conservatism of enthusiasts for the social gospel,† the retreat of ministers into preoccupation with psychiatry or with "liturgies, antiphonals and processionals." As against a dangerous European and American "dialectical theology" or "theology of crisis" he would urge adoption of a worldwide "ethical religion" and of a true "social gospel."

---

* Note that economists today testify to this fact as they describe the so-called "monopolistic competition." Ware and Means in *The Modern Economy in Action* (1936), argue that piecemeal planning in an essentially unplanned economy increases chaos rather than reducing it.

† Ward attacks the "social gospel" because it is devoted only to a short-sighted, compromising program of social service and innocuous religious education. *Which Way Religion?* pp. 30–31.

The final chapter posits the arresting query, "Is it too late?" We must avoid the new crop of false religions, he charges, those of science, Communism, Nationalism and prosperity. The vital "religion of tomorrow" must unite "mankind in common action against the common ills of life" making for "realization of all its possibilities." There is a frequent use of the phrase "the new social order" or the "Great Society." "Man as species is now struggling into organic life, reaching out his mind and hands to make the Great Society." "The nature of the new world order required by the joint demands of the machine and the rising masses is such that it needs new faith to bring it to birth" (pp. 212 f.). The closing paragraphs contain a touching appeal to the enlightened religious groups in our churches, under the conviction that "it is in the undeveloped capacities of that minority in our churches who have the vision of an ethical religion, along with the desire to realize it, that the future of American Protestantism lies hidden" (p. 221).

2. Ward's Christian Marxism

The stubborn persistence of a laissez-faire American capitalism, a world-wide paralysis of economic institutions, disappointment and confusion over the New Deal, the specter of chronic unemployment, progressive disintegration of the League of Nations, the triumph of fascism in Europe and its threat in the United States, and the rising star of the U.S.S.R.—all must have contributed to his final break with the politics and institutional framework of capitalist society.* He thus became an undisguised admirer of Marxism in its realistic political theory, as well as in its embodiment in the creative forces of the Soviet culture. His major writings from then on assumed a form which combined description of the nature and challenge of the Communist experiment with an endeavor to apply the insights, perspectives and values of Marxism to the problem of economic and political reconstruction in America. His keen interest in the new col-

* For Ward this was almost inevitably a logical step as he had been developing for two decades an increasing moral fury against the acquisitive, competitive ethos which constituted the basic drive in American life.

lectivist order was not here just being born of course; for he had made a trip to Russia in 1924 to study the so-called New Economic Policy following the period of ruthless War Communism. Moreover, with great sympathy he had usually referred to the Bolshevik Revolution and to its issue in a novel society. He wrote, for instance, in this same year that "it is to Russia that we must turn for light, for there a determined group of men used the accidental opportunity to acquire political power to attempt revolutionary economic changes which they thought would remove the causes of poverty and ignorance and make culture universal." [9]

The two volumes containing a classic statement of his enthusiasm for Sovietism are *In Place of Profit* (1933), and *The Soviet Spirit* (1944).[10] It is perhaps inadvisable to attempt a review of the details of the works. In the first place it is impossible to present here even a digest of the huge collection of factual details recorded; and in the second place the basic thesis is extraordinarily simple. To Ward the Soviet culture is exactly the opposite of the capitalist culture—that is, opposite in its fundamental orientation, tendencies and motivations. He does not, of course, regard the contemporary patterns as a final achievement, but only as "the transition between capitalism and communism," which incidentally is a genuinely orthodox Marxist idea. The claim is made that "there is no such rigidity as we are accustomed to in the social and political structure of capitalist society. What is constant is the general direction and the guiding principles, but even these are regarded as in process of development."[11] In the more recent book he charges that we in the West have always misunderstood the strength and purpose of the new order. That is why most interpretations of Soviet politics have been erroneous. Even the "experts were false prophets" who could not comprehend the "new spirit, new motives, and a growing understanding of the objectives and machinery of social-economic planning." [12] That is why also the power of resistance to the Nazi thrust was such a miracle to the English-speaking world!

In the Russia of today, Ward contends, we observe the passing of an ancient, unjust and no longer workable order. Here we come face to face with the actual demonstration that a collectivist society can be created. In Sovietism the people rule, the people take the initiative.

Although the literal beginnings of action are prompted by "the most energetic and able and intelligent," a process is set in motion by which "the masses have new opportunities to express initiative and, as controllers of the machinery and processes by which they live, to become the makers of their destiny." [13] Here we have a "government of the workers, by the workers, and for the workers." [14] The ethos of this people is different, is phenomenal, Ward boasts: "They make no claim to be a master race, entitled to rule, to plunder, to exploit. They cannot understand our racial discrimination. They have been taught the equality of all peoples; to desire a working fellowship with all other workers." [15]

The marvelous fact about Russia, he claims, is that it is a new society with a new free spirit—the spirit of work, creativity, unity, equality, security for masses, nobility of aim, devotion to human values. Hence it is a true democracy. Yet Ward does not really insist that Communism is a democracy, politically speaking. He only raises questions about the party and the government in relation to the people, asking is this a "servile state" or is the state "repressive," or what is the connection between "the party and the masses"? His answer is that it is a people's government, that the Marxist principles call for a temporary dictatorship which is bound to disappear because "to thus change it is one aspect of the continuing revolution which Communist theory and practice encourages them (the masses) to carry on." [16] He remarks also that the "Soviet Union is demonstrating in its economic management what Abraham Lincoln once said, that democracy is the people governing themselves." [17] And since "the survival of democracy anywhere in the world depends upon the extension of its principles and methods to the field of economic activities," the experience of the U.S.S.R. is contributing "to the historic line of democratic development." [18]

Perhaps the one aspect of Russian society which inspires Ward more than anything else is its repudiation of the profit incentive. The title of the first book on the U.S.S.R. is indicative of this. The profit motive is now replaced by the service motive. In an article titled "The Future of the Profit Motive"—which incidentally is an illuminating piece of economic analysis—he points out that in the strains and stresses of war, as well as in the gigantic postwar demands, there is an inescapable drive toward general planning. The "principle of service" is becoming a necessity, and "can now be developed through general planning for the common need." Such a necessity for coordination and economic planning and the lofty ideal of service now "meet at the crossroads of history." "A light to make plain this road has come down through the centuries into our hands. Our task is to hold that light so high that all who now grope in darkness, even to the ends of the earth, may see it and know which way to go." [19]

As indicated above, it is in *Democracy and Social Change* that his political outlook is best revealed. It is here too that the Marxist perspective is displayed in all its fullness. Here the moral fury against capitalist culture is maintained. Although the revolutionary has become visibly fearful of governmental power, admitting that we must preserve our "democratic tradition," the charge is made that the profit-seeking economy is experiencing a "breakdown." Capitalism in the United States is doomed; it is inefficient; it has failed to achieve the American dream; it is a moral incubus destroying the very ideals it professes to create; it has stopped at political democracy without carrying us on to true economic democracy. In Chapter V, titled "Capitalism and Democracy," he argues that historically capitalism and democracy emerged together, the former using democratic principles to destroy feudalism. But the two are inherently incompatible, the profit economy being essentially aristocratic, monopolistic, class-minded. Thus democracy and capitalism are getting further and further apart, especially in America. The breakdown of the economy shows that capitalism has failed, being incapable of meeting the full needs of all the people. But it will not give up. The present crisis is a struggle in which one or the other must suffer eclipse. Either democracy will win, destroying aristocratic capitalism and establishing a true economic equality, or capitalism will erase the last traces of the democratic political superstructure. The fight is already under way.*

Ward's attitude toward New Dealism and fascism, as well as

---

* This is basically a Marxian analysis applied to the American scene, but without the orthodox Marxian temptation to feel that victory for the new revolutionary order is somehow inevitable.

his general outlook on the nature of the state, is at bottom a Marxist approach. He assumes that the existing American government is a class instrument, the system of checks and balances having been erected "to protect the property rights of rising merchants, bankers, shipowners and landowners" (p. 63). The New Deal shows that "under the pressures of capitalistic imperialism, the real power to make war has passed into the hands of the State Department and the White House" (p. 67). Assuming that Roosevelt's domestic and foreign policies were programs of a desperate moribund capitalism, he views the existing American state as a tool of the upper wealthy classes. He warns against the illusion that the American government is not class-controlled, or that it is truly democratic, saying that to strengthen this capitalist structure will lead to totalitarianism. (p. 115). He suggests as a procedure the weakening of this fascist-minded politics while destroying the economic classes. An economically united society then can build a genuinely representative democratic state.*

In an article in *The Protestant* (August–September, 1943), titled "It is Time to Fight," Ward shows the profound influence of Marxism as he reacts to Harold Laski's argument in the latter's *Reflections on the Revolution of Our Time*. In his critique he accuses Laski of confusion, self-contradiction and of over-emphasis on the intellectual approach to revolution. Next he praises the English political theorist for a genuine socialist analysis of current conditions, trends and demands: for recognition of the decline of capitalism necessitating revolution, of need for fighting counter-revolutionary fascism, of need for decisive action at this strategic moment, for praise of Russia as a new prophetic civilization.† He finally calls the proposal in these "reflections" a "bomb without a fuse" because Laski hesitates in the presence of a demand for unwavering action, vascillates on Russia between "damnation and laudation," is tempted

* Ward links Roosevelt's action against W.P.A. sit-down strikes with the FBI, the Dies Committee, et al. as examples of those who "need and want to prevent" change (p. 104). For other instances of his feeling that Roosevelt and the New Deal were essentially tools for the defense of capitalism see *Democracy and Social Change*, pp. 73, 74, 79, 130.

† In the context Ward remarks about Sovietism: Its "rise to power marks the beginning of the socialist period of history."

in seeking "revolution by consent" to advocate a revolution which "protects privilege."

Even from this sketchy account of Ward's arguments and theories one can see that he is almost an unqualified Marxist. Yet his radical socialism is joined to a defense of democratic procedures and religious idealism.[20] Moreover, he makes the avowed claim of revising Marx, as if this is what the master social analyst himself would wish.[21] He confesses that the destruction of capitalist class society will not immediately destroy class distinctions, though the "main base of the enemy is destroyed." Again, the inevitable victory of the workers "rests more on faith than on evidence." Nor was Marx fully aware of the growing economic strength of the lower middle-class, he submits.[22] There are still other passages which would tend to show that Ward was aware of the limitations of orthodox Marxist theory; but these qualifications do not actually shake his deep, half-mystical faith in the messianic rôle of Communism.

Hardly a better revelation of his fundamental attitude can be found than that in Chapters IX and X of *Democracy and Social Change*.[23] Here is offered a suggestive analysis of the aims, objectives and ethos of Communism, especially as contrasted with fascism. The conception of democracy is set forth in terms of human values and social goals rather than in terms of institutions and processes. The contention is made that democratic methods and procedures are not dependent on the two-party system, parliamentary traditions, and uncontrolled economic processes (the free market) so characteristic of Western democracies. For the essence of democracy is the "people" in power (majority rule) and the absence of a class-divided society with its inequalities of resources and opportunities. Here is a touch of naïveté and utopianism in the assumption that the "nature of society" will be changed—all class divisions and exploitation removed—by a rearrangement of social institutions and by the creation of a "scientific economy" under a socialist state. With all his radical, apparently realistic politics Ward retains the typical social gospel faith in the unbounded capacity of man to take his collective life into his hands and create some utopia on earth.

7

Dialectical Theological Socialism: Reinhold Niebuhr

1. *The Problem of Understanding and Appraising Niebuhr*

THERE ARE many reasons why it is next to impossible to give an adequate appraisal of the position of Reinhold Niebuhr whether in theological circles or in the broad stream of contemporary American thought. In the first place he is a quite recent phenomenon—and is still in process. His thinking is in fermentation in all its aspects, despite the fact that its broad outlines can be seen with some degree of clarity. It is true that his enduring social emphases are now unmistakable, as well as the contours of a novel theological doctrine. Likewise many of the baffling dilemmas with which he wrestles are being felt increasingly by the most discerning religious spirits of our time. But what new turns his reflections may take, theologically or politically, cannot be forecast. At least it is perhaps not very safe to do so.

Another factor making Niebuhr's position difficult to characterize is that while he is widely regarded as a chief spokesman for social Christianity, that is, for the vigorous application of religious ideas to public issues, he is also generally recognized as the most powerful opponent of the social gospel idealism. Although as a rule he does not overtly attack the social gospel movement per se, certainly not its practical program, he minces no words in assaults on what we have referred to as the social gospel mentality.[1]

Still a third confusing item is Niebuhr's ambiguous relation to the so-called Neo-orthodox or Neo-Protestant movement, whether viewed in its European or American forms. While deeply influenced by the Crisis Theology—and specifically by Kierkegaard, Barth, Brunner and Tillich—he is an independently creative mind, regarded neither by himself nor by others as a follower of any European theologian. Nor is his point of view a mere variation of Anglican, Catholic or Lutheran social Christianity. As for the United States, he is at once the chief symbol of an apparently neo-supernaturalistic philosophical theology and of a radical socialist politics, but with numerous admirers who subscribe unqualifiedly neither to his theology nor to his politics.* That Niebuhr is a disturbing social force hardly any sympathetic student of his doctrines and influence could gainsay. He is perhaps the most respected and provocative, and possibly the most misunderstood, theological thinker on the American scene today. As a tribute to the vitality, originality, and influence of his ideas he was selected to deliver the famed Gifford Lectures at the University of Edinburgh for 1939, which lectures were published subsequently in two volumes (in 1941 and 1943 respectively) under the general title, *The Nature and Destiny of Man*.[2]

It is well at this point to note that Niebuhrianism and American Neo-orthodoxy are not synonymous. This is true whether one looks at the economic and political thought involved, or merely at the theological question.† There seems to be little evidence that Niebuhr's

---

* This assertion would apply even to the members of The Fellowship of Socialist Christians, a movement of which he is the principal inspiration. Its "Statement of Principles" does not demand of adherents either a liberal or a Neo-orthodox theology. Nor does it require a particular brand of socialism, a "doctrinaire" socialism. It is first and foremost a religious fellowship, not a political action group.

† The Swedish theologian George Hammar made a truly illuminating observation when he wrote: "To the *right* of Niebuhr, so to speak, there stands a group of American theologians who represent a neo-supernaturalism in its more Barthian form, and to the *left* of Niebuhr we find a large group of American theologians who have a seemingly neo-supernaturalistic program but actually have only reconstructed liberal theology or not as yet carried out their

symbolical or mythological interpretation and application of historic Christian dogma is being widely adopted. Perhaps its implication has not as yet fully dawned upon a religious world so steeped in the assumptions of naturalism and so strongly influenced by the rationalistic negations of liberalism. And certainly his robust political realism, still deeply affected by Marxian perspectives, has not as yet aroused enthusiastic endorsement, particularly since—as we shall soon see—Niebuhr himself is far from indicating with preciseness the relationship between "Christian faith" or "Christianity" and radical political doctrine and action.

A fourth element to consider in the task of gaining perspective about Niebuhr is that he is a quite unorthodox character in regard to the pattern of the "theologian." In the conventional sense he is hardly a "systematic" theologian either in the presentation of subject-matter or in the process of his intellectual growth. Davies most appropriately has emphasized this fact. His literary productions, like himself, are a strange and at times baffling mixture. He is at once theological teacher, philosopher, journalist, and political strategist. One hardly knows what to call his writings—whether philosophical reflections on the nature of man, scholarly defenses of "realistic" social theory, disquisitions on Christian ethics, or a theological critique of contemporary culture and institutions. Perhaps they are all these things, for most of his books are a fusion of elements of religious dogma, ethical idealism, preaching, philosophical criticism and political speculation. Whether he is primarily a theologian or a social philosopher is an open question.*

A fifth item making for difficulty in judging Niebuhr's significance is the paradoxical fact that he is endlessly active in secular affairs but vigorously critical of secularist social theory and secularist politics. Some observers are inclined to believe that there is no necessary

_____

vague program in any definite theology." *Christian Realism in Contemporary American Theology* (1940), p. 63.

* As a journalist Niebuhr is a provocative, incisive political commentator and critic. Besides being chief editor of *Christianity and Society* (formally *Radical Religion*) and *Christianity and Crisis*, he is a member of the editorial staff of *The Nation*, as well as having been so connected with the now defunct *The World Tomorrow*.

connection between his radical social action and his supernatural-istic, perfectionist love ethic. Moreover, his loyalties and strategies have taken on impressive changes. It became necessary to abandon the pacifist Fellowship of Reconciliation and the Socialist Party of America, as well as to tone down the Christian Marxist emphasis of the early thirties. He has remained vigorous in his political and journalistic "radicalism," while concentrating more and more upon the religious Fellowship of Socialist Christians which engages pri-marily in educational, devotional and charitable activities. His im-mediate aims seem to be indistinguishable from those of a well-known political reformism, while he spares no pains to reveal his aversion to "doctrinaire" socialism and to (for him) star-gazing hopes such as, for example, plans for world government or pro-letarian revolution. Certainly in referring to his "movement to the right" theologically and "movement to the left" politically one cannot depend upon a conventional application of these phrases.[3]

A sixth factor in the matter of understanding Niebuhr is the much-discussed "dialectical" method. The term dialectic has a variety of meanings historically. In the days of Socrates, Plato and Aristotle —the word is Greek in origin—it meant popularly "discussion," "de-bate," or "conversation," but became refined to mean a technique of reasoning or argumentation. Hegel gave it a special signification in his speculations, namely, the means of logically arriving at truth and reality by development of conflicting truths, the process lead-ing to ever higher truths. His famous over-all formula, thesis, antith-esis and synthesis, is one of the best known logical frameworks in the history of philosophy. Few patterns of thought have had wider influence in modern times than "Hegelian dialectics." More recently, however, religious thinkers have been applying the term with a unique theological connotation. These past uses are not a simple clue to "dialectical" theological method; yet the new use is in some respects a variation or fresh application. Dialectical theol-ogy is logical in method and is preoccupied with the conflict element in truth and reality. It pursues truth by concentrating on conflicting opposites.

Though Niebuhr's views as we noted are not a mere replica of European or British patterns, he is a genuine thinker of the dialectical type. As Professor Bennett has put it, and very aptly, Dr. Niebuhr's approach involves "the preservation of opposing tendencies in a state of tension."[4] He has exposed his mind to the most complex and contradictory ideas in politics, ethics, theology and philosophy. Intellectually he is a man of many lives and moods, defending and attacking at some point or another practically every system of thought to which he has given serious attention. It is difficult to prove that he belongs to any particular school. His Neo-orthodox theology is most unorthodox, whether compared with historic Christian orthodoxy or liberal theology. His socialism is as much a rational assault upon it as it is a defense of its necessity. Pacifism he reasons against as a political technique, while justifying it as an expression of transcendent Christian idealism. He utilizes the perspectives of Marx, yet renounces Marxism almost furiously. Orthodox Christianity, particularly in its American "fundamentalist" form, seems to him an utterly bankrupt tradition. But he would return to its insights, doctrines and truths which, though expressed by him in an unconventional mythical form, offer a key to the ultimate meaning of God, history and human destiny. Amidst all the complexity of his descriptions, criticisms and philosophic reflections he refuses to do violence to any facet of truth by insisting on uncompromising logical consistency. For him, apparently no truth must be rejected because of its outmoded form, and no outmoded form need be accepted merely because it contains a grain of truth.

A seventh cause of confusion in Niebuhr's expositions, aside from his complex dialectical treatment of all sorts of problems, situations and theories, is that the expositor has the habit of utilizing numerous words, phrases and concepts whose meanings are not sharply defined in such a manner as to remove honest confusion on the part of the reader. The confusion is further heightened by his tendency to generalize and universalize, by a flare for sharp and superlative statements, and by a love for paradox. Add to this his remarkable capacity for sensing the grain of truth in almost any system of thought or pattern of social action, together with his insistence on doing full justice to such truth as is found, and one finds himself hard up against the almost impossible task of interpreting his views without doing violence to them in some of their aspects.

Let us observe just three very crucial terms which he employs throughout most of his literary products, terms by no means given in an unambiguous sense. Such are democracy, Christianity (or Christian) and utopianism (or utopian). Note, for example, the way in which he uses "democracy" and "democratic" in *The Children of Light and the Children of Darkness*. Democracy is a "historic ideal and institution" with "ephemeral" and "valid" elements. It is both an "ideal" and a "perennially valuable form of social organization." It cannot, however, be "equated with freedom" since it must maintain freedom within the "framework of order." He so applies democracy as to make British and American societies, for example, true democracies, yet outmoded because of "middle-class ideology." He then turns to the Marxists and labels them "children of light" because they have a type of democracy, believing in a law higher than themselves. In fact he repeatedly lumps Marxism and bourgeois ideology together under the "social philosophy of democratic civilization" (pp. 6–7). Again he refers to "democratic theory, whether in its liberal or its more radical form" (p. 33), as if Marxism is merely a form of democracy corrupted by its "sentimental" creed. To sum up: Niebuhr uses democracy sometimes as if it were an abstract ideal or a set of human values, sometimes as if it were a certain form of organization and process to be distinguished from the tyrannies of the "children of darkness," sometimes as if it were a social philosophy tainted with an "optimistic creed."

Space being short, we dare not discuss his employment of "Christianity" and "Christian" in detail. He frequently uses "Christianity" as if it meant the historically faithful portrayal of it or of some aspect of it. Again he speaks of it in a sort of sociological sense as "liberal Christianity," "Christian orthodoxy," the "Christian heritage," "modern Christianity," the "conflict between Christianity and Communism." He is willing, for instance, to defend Western democratic "Christian" civilization against the threat of an avowedly anti-Christian Nazism, as he declared editorially in 1941 in the opening issue of *Christianity and Crisis*. But very often he means by Christianity only "true" Christianity as he himself expounds it. This is what is implied when he calls modern forms of Christian pacifism "heretical," going on further to deny that "even the most democratic structure of justice can be 'Christian.'"[5] It can be seen even from this brief statement that a general clarification, in a critical sense, of what he means when he employs such words would be helpful to the careful student in regard to a given context in which his views are expounded.

Few words appear more frequently in Niebuhr's works than utopian and utopianism, often in connection with "illusion," "romanticism," "optimism" or "sentimentality." Despite this fact, the nature of utopianism as he strikes at it in various forms—among secular and religious liberals, among Marxists, rationalists, idealists—is not too precisely indicated in every connection. It is not that Niebuhr's general trend of thought is obscure; for nothing could be more vivid than the fact that he hurls his shafts at false ideas, theories and programs which do not correspond to "reality" or to the requirement for effectiveness. Sometimes he rejects them because they distort the total body of truth. In one respect he no doubt means by "utopianism" what Marx signified by "ideology," namely, illusory, delusional and therefore ultimately futile, self-defeating thinking.* But this general notion of false, unreal or illusory ideas and doctrines does not seem to describe adequately the particular shades of thought under attack by him. Or to put it another way, we cannot always discern easily just why he is inclined to picture a specific proposal or body of theory as "utopian." For instance, Marxism for him is often regarded as political "realism." Yet nothing has he underscored more often or more heavily than the "romantic elements in Marxism," showing that this body of ideas is a perfect example of modern utopianism. Indeed, it is just another sentimental "optimistic creed." †

* With Marx, of course, "ideology" also involved an unconscious defense of the status quo as the "ideological" thinker was always deeply influenced by the limited perspectives of his social environment or by class interests.

† In *Reflections on the End of an Era* he gives to Chapter XV the title of "The Political Realism of Christian Orthodoxy." Thus two systems of ideas ordinarily thought to be at opposite poles, Marxism and Christian Orthodoxy, are both regarded as politically "realistic." In his strictures on "idealists" who hope for "world community" one is not always sure as to whether these hopes are romantic because idealists expect such community or merely expect it without realistic procedures. Cf. for instance, *The Nature and Destiny of Man*, II, 284 f.

It might not do violence to Niebuhr's fundamental outlook at this point to say that for him the essence of utopianism seems to be *false expectation,* an inability to see the real connections between present circumstances, present proposals, or present beliefs and one's projected hopes. In some instances the present circumstances may be such as almost certainly to defeat the projected hopes if they were undertaken. In other instances the idealistic proposals, if actually attempted, would result in unsuspected degrading compromises or in cruelties and injustices which in the end would be discouraging to the would-be progressives. There are apparently three ways in which a given idea, program or policy may be utopian in Niebuhr's thinking:

1. In the sense that were it actually executed it would bring results far different from those anticipated.
2. In the sense that, given present conditions, resources and means it is evidently impossible to achieve.
3. In the sense that proposed policies or techniques fail to meet the central issue or problem in the situation.

Here finally we may observe that Niebuhr's peculiar brand of "Christian realism," in the light of repeated use of such an ambiguous term as "utopianism," lays itself open to gross misinterpretation. For he is a special type of religious idealist himself despite his charges against the illusions of idealists, liberals, moralists and fanatical Marxists. Utopianism for him is not the possession or pursuit of absolutist goals—which he cherishes himself though not expecting their realization on the historical plane—but the unconscious identification of these goals with "proximate solutions" and with past or present cultural achievements. Though he condemns a Lenin for "provisional cynicism," he himself possesses a provisional pessimism. His theories, "dialectically" speaking, provide for somber religious "realism," a sense of tragic frustration and defeat in this present world (like early Christian apocalypticism and contemporary Christian orthodoxy) combined with an ultimate optimism, an imperishable hope of redemption beyond this place of wrath and tears. Between this immediate "despair" and ultimate "hope" he would apply in the interim of the earthly human drama "realistic" political theories and tactics. But the language he employs in the welter of analysis and speculation, the many key words and concepts, frequently puzzle even the careful reader.*

2. *The First Phase of Niebuhr's Social Thought*

A close observation of Dr. Niebuhr's political and economic views enables one to see two important phases aside from the rather inchoate liberal social reformism of the early twenties. From about 1930 roughly to 1934–35 he veered strongly to the left, becoming positively socialist. His socialism became virtually identical with a Christian Marxism. The key books reflecting the move toward this position are *The Contribution of Religion to Social Work, Moral Man and Immoral Society* and *Reflections on the End of an Era.*[6] The second phase of Niebuhr's political thought is a movement somewhat to the right of this Marxist emphasis, although the influence of Marxism is still pronounced in his thinking. In later books, beginning with *An Interpretation of Christian Ethics* in 1935 and running through *The Children of Light and the Children of Darkness* in 1944, his aversion to Marxism and proletarian revolution is quite pronounced. At the same time his system of ideas received a new expression within the context of a dialectical theology —with a marked effect upon his political and economic outlook. A good index to the change may be gained by comparing critically the tone of *Reflections on the End of an Era* with that of *The Children of Light and the Children of Darkness,* produced exactly ten years later.

Let us look more closely at the details of his arguments, analyses and interpretations to see whether this general conclusion is justified. By 1930 Niebuhr had become thoroughly disillusioned with liberal

* In a remarkable passage at the close of *Moral Man and Immoral Society* Niebuhr uses the word "illusion" as he often does "utopianism," and refers to the "myth" of perfect justice as a "very valuable illusion for the moment," as an effective agent in the task of redemption. Here "illusion" is equivalent to "utopia" as employed in Mannheim's *Ideology and Utopia,* the utopian thinker being a realistic explosive social force, the real challenger of the status quo. Thus may not proletarian illusions be "utopian" and "realistic" at the same time, even in Niebuhr's reasoning?

social reformism.* He was overwhelmed by the appalling injustices evident everywhere in modern industrial civilization, and particularly by the concentration of power and resources in the hands of a relatively small wealthy class. Economic power, he declared, in modern society has "become the source of more injustice than any other, because the private ownership of the productive processes and the increased centralization of the resultant power in the hands of a few, make inevitably for irresponsibility." [7] Adequate housing for the poor "can never be initiated within the limits of private enterprise." Social work itself accepts "philanthropy as a substitute for real justice," and though it pretends to be scientific is really little better than the "most sentimental religious generosity." [8] Irresponsible power leads inevitably to injustice "no matter how intelligent the person who wields it." Hence the real problem cannot be solved by increasing social intelligence and humanitarian sentiments, but "only by setting the power of the exploited against the exploiters." In industrial society "equalitarianism becomes a more and more compelling social philosophy" because of inequality which periodically results in economic chaos. And though the workers may in due time "develop a social strategy which will horrify every middle-class idealist," it is to the modern proletarian that "the future in an industrial civilization undoubtedly belongs." [9]

In these early years of the depression Niebuhr became an unqualified socialist, without hesitation expressing his radicalism in positive, practical, political terms. He was an ardent supporter of the Socialist Party of America, as well as a chief organizer and protagonist for the Fellowship of Socialist Christians. This latter move-

* Indeed, when he wrote *Does Civilization Need Religion?* (1927), he had already become sharply critical of a tendency toward "conservatism" in liberal Christianity. See in this volume for example Chapter IV titled "The Social Conservatism of Modern Religion." Thus even in the mid-twenties his break had begun with the social gospel mentality, as well as with a political conservatism based on a middle-class outlook inherited from historic Protestantism. In fact, his experience as a young pastor in Detroit during the war and the early postwar years created in him a disturbing disillusionment in regard to a Christian society professing to be built upon capitalist industrialism such as he saw it illustrated by the Ford enterprise. Cf. his *Leaves from the Notebook of a Tamed Cynic.*

[114]

ment, to whose purposes he heartily subscribed, declared at the time of its organization in 1932 that among its aims one was the support of "the Socialist Party or such other party as may embody the purposes of socialism as the political organization most nearly approximating a political expression of Christian ethics for our day." (Number seven in the list of announced objectives).

When *Moral Man and Immoral Society* appeared in 1932–33 it dropped like a bombshell upon educators, social scientists, politicians and religious idealists alike. It was widely interpreted as a sample of the growing social pessimism of our era.[10] While there may still be disputes as to the implications of its thesis or as to the place the work holds in the development of the political outlook of its author, some central emphases are unquestionable. Here Niebuhr's disillusionment with the possibility of an ideal society and his acceptance of the inevitability of inter-group conflict run like threads through the whole. Individuals, he argues, may have lofty sentiments and noble intentions; they may in personal relationships do commendable work which is a real blessing to the community. But collective man—man as he acts through classes, races, nations, political parties —is essentially "immoral." The struggle among these vast associations of human beings is mainly a matter of power rather than of morality. While intimate, more or less personal contacts are not exclusively ethical, and while inter-group relations are not exclusively political (that is, governed by pressures), the non-ethical character of human action increases as one moves out into these areas of large collectivities.

Nowhere else has his reputed pessimism been more clearly displayed. He asserts that "it is safe to hazard the prophecy that the dream of perpetual peace and brotherhood for human society is one which will never be fully realised" (p. 21). Though human beings are naturally selfish and unselfish, and though "growing rationality is a guarantee of man's growing morality," and though individuals may be sincerely devoted to a cause or community, "the will to power remains" (p. 46). Hence we must accept the "rather pathetic" fact that in our kind of world "conflict is a seemingly unavoidable prerequisite of group solidarity" (p. 48). On "the morality of nations," he avers that nations are held together "more by force and emotion, than by mind." True internationalists, men really possessed of universal rather than national loyalties, "must always remain a minority group." American hypocrisy in the Spanish-American War, the tactics of the British Government in building an empire, the lofty religious pretensions of a "Holy Alliance" by Austria, Prussia and Russia, the vindictive spirit in the Treaty of Versailles, our dubious motives in passing the Japanese Exclusion Act, the veiled quest for power behind the maneuverings of the League of Nations and of the Disarmament Conference—all these and many more facts could be cited to show that there is not enough intelligence and morality in the world to bring "effective social restraint upon the self-will of nations, at least not upon the powerful nations" (p. 111).

Continuing his gloomy observations by examining the morality of "privileged classes" and that of "the proletarian class," he concludes that "rational and moral resources" may "only qualify," but not "destroy the selfishness of classes." The significance of Marxism is that it shows "the brutalities of the conflict of power as basic to the collective history of mankind" (pp. 154 f.). He further indicates the Marxist tinge in his thinking by declaring that the root of social injustice is "disproportion of power in society" (p. 163). In this context Niebuhr utters a classic phrase when he charges that the middle-class world lacks perspective enough to sense the justice of the workers' cause, steeped as that world is "in petty virtues and major vices." Proletarian class loyalty, devotion to the equalitarian ideal, is thus nobler than a narrow patriotism. Despite the claims of the nation, "there is no reason why a class which is fated by its conditions of life to aspire after an equalitarian society should not have a high moral claim upon the loyalty of its members." If national devotion seems to be more worthy, "that is only because traditional sentiments overpower rational considerations" (p. 227). Though at one place he pleads for increase in the "human imagination" of a "labor movement which is not completely disinherited," he is not sure that the way of proletarian revolution can be avoided ultimately. In any case revolution is morally justified wherever it is an absolute political necessity. "The contrasting virtues and vices of revolutionary and evolutionary socialism," he contends, "are such

[116]

that no purely rational moral choice is possible between them" (p. 230).

It must not be assumed, nevertheless, that his strong affection for the proletarian cause renders him uncritical of socialism in *Moral Man and Immoral Society*. Socialism in both its Marxist and Revisionist forms is flayed by him repeatedly. He notes that Marxism is one of the tragic expressions of "modern man's loss of confidence in moral forces." While middle-class morality is a manifestation of hypocrisy and sentimentality, proletarian class morality is poisoned with brutality and cynicism (p. 177). Moreover, the Marxian dogma about the inevitability of revolution is a delusion.* Thrusts are made at the Communist belief in the goodness of human nature, and warnings given of an almost certain political corruption following revolution. Speaking of "justice through political force," he has just as little sympathy for the hopes and strategies of British and Continental Revisionist Socialism as he has for orthodox Marxist illusions. After tracing gains of evolutionary socialism (pp. 206–209), he then becomes so unimpressed by its prospects for the future that he places his "realism" right back on a Marxian perspective, being doubtful of "radical economic change" without revolution and attacking British socialists for unqualified confidence in the "parliamentary method" (p. 209).

A striking aspect of this work is the rather odd presentation in its pages of a sharply radical socialist theory about political conditions and processes in combination with a vast, almost philosophical pessimism about the total human enterprise. The juxtaposition of Marxist analyses with a somber perspective upon the drama of history in fact remained as a permanent feature of his thinking. The same elements of socialist theory and historical pessimism, with the addition of an absolutist religious ethic, became the leading threads in his next outstanding book.

In *Reflections on the End of an Era* the Christian Marxist point

* See pp. 181–91 where Niebuhr realistically portrays the conditions which led to revolution in Russia, along with the special situations in other Western countries where the repetition of the revolutionary pattern becomes highly improbable.

of view reaches its climax, its most complete expression. Moreover, the mood of gloom, the malaise about society, is very intense.* George Hammar says that Niebuhr in this book "becomes a pessimistic American Spengler," tragically viewing modern civilization as destroying itself.[11] It is true that the opening pages sound very Spenglerian, with a Neo-Freudian view of human nature reinforcing the historical perspective. Impulse is the driving power in society. Reason is paramount too, but its force is largely that of strengthening (or rather directing and justifying) impulse. Rationality becomes a means of self-deception even in the highest cultures. Hence modern civilization is doomed to conflict, anarchy, as impulse or the will-to-power finally triumphs over reason and moral idealism. Yet it is only in the first chapter, titled "The Life and Death of Civilizations," that his "reflections" take on this Schopenhauer-like melancholy. Elsewhere throughout the book the analysis of political and economic processes takes the form of a Christian Marxism.

Capitalism is doomed. "It must therefore give way to a new social system which is better fitted to organize life under new conditions" (p. 32). Thus the capitalist economy has outlived its usefulness. It is an instrument of inequality and injustice, and must ultimately perish by its own processes. Indeed it generates out of itself the forces of destruction. The "social struggle in America" [12] is set forth in strictly Marxist terms. Although capitalism is breaking down, the issues in America are confused, and labor is not yet mature in understanding and organization. Decades may be required for a sharpening of the struggle; but the trends are clear. Even if the "ultimate crisis" does not come until the "end of the century," the conflict will continue to deepen and will finally issue in a situation in which capitalism and socialism each sharpens "its own position in a process of standing in unqualified juxtaposition to the other" (p. 81). The New Deal is here regarded by Niebuhr as a vague, un-

* Yet it is just in this book that the profoundly religious tone, the foreshadowing of a Christian Neo-orthodoxy, makes its unmistakable appearance. The revolutionary is now quite horrified at the "peril of barbarism in the spirit of vengeance," pleads for a "radical political theory" qualified by a "religious ethic," for an "unprudential passion for perfect rationality," and concludes with a chapter titled "The Assurance of Grace," an essay containing the germ of a coming dialectical mythological theology.

stable state capitalism which is a preliminary to fascism. The failure of its program will generate two contradictory forces: reactionism and political radicalism. The final result, however long the process, can be only conflict and ultimate overthrow of the existing order. For there can be no gradual transition from laissez-faire capitalism through state capitalism to genuine socialism.*

But his Marxism is most clearly revealed in the interpretation of fascism as "the class struggle in its final desperate stages." It is the last stage of a dying capitalism which becomes desperate and destroys the remnants of democracy in a frantic effort to check its dissolution. The unity of the fascist state is artificial, combining conservative and radical elements held together by force and oppression. But revolution is possible even if no destructive war is initiated. A war, however, means the almost certain internal defeat of the capitalist-fascist movement, for the oppressed proletarians are likely to turn the occasion into a civil war to overthrow the financial and industrial oligarchs who are manipulating the state for their purposes.

In the latter half of the book, particularly from Chapter XIII on, the Christian insights are fused with Marxian ideas. Here Niebuhr seems to approach a revolutionary Christian socialism, a revised Marxism purged of illusions, of ruthless iconoclasm and bungling tactics. He urges that with the development of a "radical political theory" there be added a religiously motivated social ethic. Three necessary ingredients, it seems to him, must form the basis for an adequate social theory and strategy: a political policy which checks conflicting egoisms in society, moral idealism and altruistic incentives, and a religious world view. He finally revolts against unqualified Marxism with its cruelty, destructiveness, fanaticism, pride, and political corruption. But the political problem is left unsolved, even from a strictly theoretical point of view. He is far from convinced that he can Christianize Marxism. If Niebuhr's faith is here anchored in the possibility of a proletarian organization and discipline, combined with highly moral leadership and a thorough educational preparation of public opinion, such as to accomplish revolution and

---

* On p. 79 Niebuhr shows how unqualified were his Marxist assumptions when he remarked that American New Dealism was a "state capitalism" promoting a labor movement "to act as a police force" for its defense.

yet reduce the inevitable destruction to a tolerable modicum, he does not say so definitely. The strictly political analyses drop away at the end of the book, being replaced by the introduction of the dialectical theology. It is his intention, however, in Chapters XIX and XX to defend the thesis that "religious disinterestedness" and faith in the grace of God have special relevance for the political problem.*

There are two brief articles written in 1934 which give further evidence of how strongly Marxist was Niebuhr's outlook during this period. One is a comment by him on a revolutionary "Appeal to the Socialist Party," published in *The World Tomorrow* of April 12. The other, carried in the same journal, issue of June 14, 1934, was given the title of "The Fellowship of Socialist Christians." The arguments and analyses in these passages are very instructive. In the first article he is pleading that the Socialist Party reject the proposal of forty-seven members who suggest that the Party transform itself into a true revolutionary movement, unite with labor, the farmer and various other groups, and lead on under a "united front" to the destruction of capitalism in America through the instrumentality of a proletarian dictatorship. Niebuhr branded this as a star-gazing plan, blindly following the Russian pattern without being "politically realistic and relevant to the American scene." But he adds significantly that "what America needs is a socialism with no illusions about the final limits of the parliamentary method." "The tragic events of the past decade," he continues, "have proved that the struggle for power is a more ruthless proposition than parliamentary revisionists believed." What we need is a "revision of Marxist thought" which, purged of dialectical materialism and suspicion of connections with Russian Communism, will lead on to final revolution, no doubt with "the temporary abrogation of democracy." But to advocate such revolution in a country which is not fully prepared, thus necessitating "the help of non-proletarian forces for its victory, is to speak without realism."

In the article dealing with "The Fellowship of Socialist Chris-

* As we can see, Niebuhr has not quite extricated himself even today from the apparently insoluble dilemma. In 1940 Hammar correctly observed that "in his ethics Niebuhr is thus torn between a radical non-Christian political program and Christian love perfectionism." *Op. cit.,* p. 224.

tians" Niebuhr uses several meaningful phrases to describe the members of this body, including himself. This is an association of "radical Christians," "Christian Socialists," "Socialist Christians," "Realistic Christian Socialists," "Christian Marxians." What these members of the Fellowship are concerned about, he declares, is not orthodox Marxism with its "historical materialism," but "the political and economic realism of Marxism." A realistic religion must reject the "excessive moralism of liberal Christianity" as well as the social pessimism of orthodoxy. "The Christian Marxian," Niebuhr argues, "has a more pessimistic view of human nature than liberal Protestantism," and thus regards social catastrophe not as "mere chaos but as a revelation of the meaning of life and a proof of the fact that the wages of sin is death and that the consequence of injustice in a civilization is the destruction of that civilization." He draws the conclusion that far-seeing, prophetic Christians—who will no doubt remain a minority in relation to the total body of Christians—may see the social problem realistically and cast their lot with "the disinherited who are fated to be the champions and the heralds of a new society." [13]

3. Dialectical Theological Socialism

Our study so far has shown that Niebuhr became completely disillusioned with rationalistic liberal theology on the one hand and its social gospel reformism on the other. However in the late twenties and early thirties his main attention was centered not on the theological question but on the politico-ethical problem. Rejecting a mild political reformism based on the assumptions of a middle-class outlook which did not challenge the deeper roots of social injustice, he was finally driven to embrace a Marxist ideology which apparently offered the key to the problem of building a new world. Marxism to him was the clue because it saw the realities of inevitable class conflict, the root of injustice in the disproportions of power and privilege inherent in the very structure of bourgeois society, the coming doom of capitalism by its own inner chaos and disintegration, the impossibility of avoiding force, even destructive violence, in a social order torn by irreconcilable economic interests, the locus of political power in the possession of property, and an organized militant proletariat as the only means for effectuating a genuine transfer of power essential for basic justice.

But at the time his preoccupation with proletarian socialism was most extreme, his doubts and dilemmas reached a fresh intensity. The new problem became that of Christianizing Marxism and adapting its essential values to the American scene. *Reflections on the End of an Era* is significant in that it expresses in bold relief this gigantic issue. While there is little indication that Niebuhr at this time saw clearly the way out, of one thing he seemed fairly sure: the insights and perspectives of Marxism must be maintained and yet Christianity cannot be abandoned! He then turned his analyses upon the theological problem and its social implications, finally emerging with a supernaturalistic "neo-orthodox" Christian dogma, with its implication for the interpretation of human nature and history. Most of his later writings—particularly *An Interpretation of Christian Ethics, Beyond Tragedy, Christianity and Power Politics* and *The Nature and Destiny of Man*—are expressions of a new struggle for the solution of the social problem by reinterpreting it within the general framework of this dialectical theology. The Weltanschauung from which he now views the perennial question of social justice is one based upon a philosophical Christian anthropology which enables him to preserve a political "realism" without surrendering either to middle-class ideologies in secularist or religious versions or to the Marxian metaphysics and philosophy of history. Thus he endeavors to erect what we choose to describe as a dialectical theological socialism.

Niebuhr's first task, therefore, in the quest for a more tenable Christian social theory (that is, a more realistic religious social ethic) is that of laying down basic philosophical principles. "A religious morality is constrained," he concludes, "by its sense of the dimension of depth to trace every force with which it deals to some ultimate origin and to relate every purpose to some ultimate end." [14] We must seek to achieve "a philosophy of human nature and destiny" which would "reach farther into the heights and depths of life than the medieval synthesis; and would yet be immune to the alternate moods of pessimism and optimism, of cynicism and of sentimentality to which modern culture is now so prone." [15] He does not hesitate to affirm that moral idealism and political doctrines should be based upon, that is, should grow out of, religious presuppositions. He declares that democracy "requires religious humility"; and that such humility "springs only from the depth of a religion which confronts the individual with a more ultimate majesty and purity than all human majesties and values." [16] He charges that modern democratic secularism is "half false" in holding the achievement of a democratic order as the ultimate social value; for man is always driven to "ask ultimate questions about the meaning of life for which there is no answer in the partial fulfillments and frustrations of the historical process." [17] The whole of the volume, *Beyond Tragedy,* is a quest for a Christian philosophy of history, a philosophy presumably relevant to the total human enterprise, as a constant struggle for justice and as a perennial "tragedy," beyond whose historical boundaries lies the hope of victory through a God of grace and love.

These ultimate religious principles and perspectives furnish the web into which is woven a new dialectical approach to the nature of man and the course of history. Man is individually and collectively a complex of contradictory impulses, desires, ideals. He is essentially creative, possessed of endless energy; but his creativity is both glorious and diabolical. The "human vitalities" are "capable of unpredictable creative and destructive consequences."* Human passion, energy, ambition and idealism possess an "indeterminate character," even in their loftiest and "most spiritualized forms"; and hence are capable of setting in motion all sorts of forces for good or evil, or rather for good *and* evil.

Hence man is basically a dual creature, that is, a creature with a dual nature. Looked at from a standpoint of nature and natural

---

* P. 47. It is impossible here to give anything approaching an adequate treatment of Niebuhr's amazingly fresh and original approach to the nature of human nature. The author must simply refer the reader to volume I of his Gifford Lectures. In our all-too-brief account of Niebuhr's *political* ideas we quote freely from *The Children of Light and the Children of Darkness* which offers some of his insights in their bearing on the immediate issues of democracy and totalitarianism.

processes, he is both a part of nature and a spirit "transcendent" over the "natural process." "The freedom of the human spirit over the natural process makes history possible" (p. 49). The deficiency of both bourgeois and Marxist social theory is just this tendency to see man merely from the conventional naturalistic viewpoint. Such theory endeavors "to understand man without considering the final dimension of his spirit" (p. 59). But man is a dual being also looked at from the standpoint of religious ethics. He is a rational and idealistic spirit, a divine creature in "the image of God," driven to seek truth, to seek absolute values and goals, perennially asking "questions about the meaning of life," and discovering his "final meaning in community." On the other hand he is a sinner, a rebel against God and the universal community. He is fundamentally proud and egoistic, endlessly employing even his most beautiful and moral ideals as self-seeking techniques, and in the very professions of humility manifesting his pride. There is a deep-seated diabolical tendency to make our "own standards the final norms of existence and to judge others for failure to conform to them" (p. 140). Again, "pride, which seeks to hide the conditioned and finite character of all human endeavor, is the very quintessence of sin" (p. 135).

Here we see the implication of a dialectical Christian anthropology for political and economic theories, as well as for racial policies. Every political creed is partly erroneous and always dangerous, even democracy, because no secular social ideal is "great enough or good enough to make itself the final end of existence" (p. 133). Hence in this respect the democratic credo is only "a less vicious version of the Nazi creed." As for economic principles, conservatives tend to mistake "some proximate solution" of the economic problem for the ultimate solution, while radicals assume that once their scheme has triumphed evil will disappear with the new property arrangements. The stupid "children of light" like the Marxists and the democratic utopians correctly perceive the need of bringing individual and group interests into a working harmony for the sake of the total community, but fail to understand how difficult of realization is this hope.

As for the "children of darkness" (or the "children of this world"), that is, the pessimists, cynics, moral nihilists (the fascists in international politics), they are realistic enough to understand the power of self-interest in human affairs. Though evil because "they know no law beyond the self," they are far wiser than the "children of light." They know how even the best of men with the noblest professions in their hearts long for power and glory, pursue their selfish ends under high-sounding symbols, and ultimately pay the biggest rewards to the successful rather than to the virtuous. Hence the fascists have played one idealistic nation against another, with none of the idealists genuinely believing, until almost too late, that international diplomacy could really be as corrupt and irrational as it appeared, or that an enlightened country like Germany could actually trust its destiny to a near-maniac like Hitler. Still less were these sentimentalists and utopians aware, as were the "children of darkness," that even the "optimism of democratic life" was itself a reflection of "the typical illusion of an advancing class which mistook its own progress for the progress of the world" (p. 2).*

In the second volume of the Gifford Lectures, Chapters IX and X are given the titles respectively of "The Kingdom of God and the Struggle for Justice" and "The End of History." Here Niebuhr shows that in the struggle for justice each achievement is an approximation to the Kingdom of God and at the same time a negation of the Kingdom. Rules and laws of justice approximate and contradict community (p. 248). He believes in "the validity of the principle of equality on the one hand and the impossibility of realizing it fully on the other" (p. 255). The general function of government is the achievement of order, stability, justice, community well-being; but it always remains in actuality both a principle of "order" and an instrument of "domination." The sin of pretension and idolatry is never absent from political life (pp. 267–269). The truly Christian approach to government is a dialectical one, regarding it as both a divine agent of order and a false pretension to majesty.[18]

* For another excellent illustration of how Niebuhr states his fundamental principles succinctly as he applies them to specific issues see the essay on "Why the Christian Church is Not Pacifist." This is published as Chapter I of his collection of essays under the general title, *Christianity and Power Politics*, 1940.

"History," he says in one of his stimulating dialectical epigrams, "moves towards the realization of the Kingdom but yet the judgment of God is upon every new realization" (p. 286).

Notice that Niebuhr has completely rejected the conventional idea of progress whether in liberal-democratic or Marxist form. While social forces move forward in ever new creation and proliferation, evil also moves forward in equally great proportions. True, our world is not a meaningless machine. Neither is the social order a growing organism. It is not an evolutionary process—continuous or dialectical—by which human culture expands toward a brotherhood on earth. Rather is human history a vast zigzag drama between Creation and the Parousia, with every point of time, as von Ranke put it, equidistant from eternity. Hence the following assumptions are basic to Niebuhr's dialectical philosophy of history:

1. There is no dogmatic affirmation about what is and what is not achievable in history; for potentialities for achievement are indeterminate.

2. But with every actual achievement there is the possibility, indeed the inevitability, of perversion, of corruption.

3. This corruption is everywhere due ultimately to an ineradicable flaw in human nature, to sin whose essence is pride, egoism, self-centeredness, the will-to-power.

4. Pride and hence corruption and social disorder become very pronounced in the aspirations of large groups such as races, nations, classes, social movements in which a sense of guilt for decisions and actions becomes immensely weakened. The ethnocentrism and ruthlessness of such collectivities can be checked only by an effective opposing force.

5. Therefore no historical utopia is possible since no approximation to justice, however ideal the accomplishment, can completely eliminate the conflict and injustice due to this persistent basic flaw in human nature.

6. Since the sin of pride persists in some degree and form on every level of achievement, such achievement becomes tentative and precarious, surrounded always with the underlying threat of a crisis which may catapult society back to the stage of barbarism.

7. The irony of man's fate, of his tragic destiny, is thus bound up with his gloriously and pathetically complex nature, as he is tempted always amidst his visions to rely upon the illusion of perfection, and thus fails periodically to assume realistically the requirements for the control of evil in a durable system of rough justice. And thus in this very illusion and negligence he adds greater assurance both to the recurrence of social catastrophe and to ultimate historical doom.

8. Even with doom in nature and history, hope is not entirely lost since the God who has revealed Himself in Christ is one of mercy and grace. In Christ He has disclosed His redemptive purposes; and hence even now we can have a foretaste of that ultimate fulfilment beyond the domain of time and place.

Perhaps the point at which Marxist thought has left its indelible impression upon the Christian dialectician is in his analysis of the relation between power and the struggle for justice. Here Niebuhr has shown a more profound understanding of the nature and significance of power than most (usually tender-minded) American political thinkers, secular and religious. His viewpoint may be summarized as follows:

1. That the struggle for social justice is always involved in a contest of power. It is never a question of mere morality versus power.
  (a) Because all contending groups lay claim to "right," to morality, giving moral justification to their position or demands.
  (b) Because men are always power-seekers, even the most moral of them. Even their "ideals" express themselves in a quest for power.
  (c) Because groups are even more concerned for power (less for morality) than individuals, and thus justice becomes a question of continual adjustment of group claims.
2. That the essence of social justice is a full consideration of the claims of all parties, with every system of justice resulting from compromise. No contending group can have all it wants or contends for, and hence must be restrained by force in its selfish aspirations.
3. That achievement of justice is dependent upon a relative equality of power (or balance of power), for
  (a) Where vast disproportions of power exist, justice is a mockery —it becomes the will of the mighty. The system of order resulting is merely the law of the ruling power which never fully considers the claims of the weaker.
  (b) Where equality of power exists all contenders get a hearing because the power of an opponent always tends to check one's pretensions and claims.
4. A structure of justice based on a balance of power is morally inferior to a community of love. But corrupt human nature will require a rough balance to the end of time. To imagine otherwise is to be victimized by illusions concerning man and social processes.

What then are the political implications of this novel dialectical theological Weltanschauung? To what extent is this Neo-orthodox

Christian interpretation of history and social processes bound up with a socialistic theory and strategy? No doubt a recent statement of the "Principles" of the Fellowship of Socialist Christians expresses Niebuhr's views in this regard. These "Principles" express a plea for a "democratically controlled economic system," and for a socialism "without the acceptance of doctrinaire blueprints for the future which are so often associated with the word." Moreover, such religious socialism, since it is but the outcome of fallible human judgments (though judgments "religiously inspired"), is not to be identified with "Christian faith." Yet conviction is strong that capitalism must break down, and a socialized economy must be built and controlled "in terms of general planning."

Here we must acknowledge that the dialectical socialism has become rather vague, attenuated, and non-committal. The fact is, this intellectual rebel centers his scholarship almost entirely upon ultimate theological, ethical and philosophical principles. In his major writings since 1934 there is virtually no speculation on questions like the practical functions of governments, the relation of government to economic life, the role of parties, various types of planning, the problem of political leadership, the status and function of organized labor, prospects for economic change, and strategy in achieving a socialist system. Even the Soviet system makes virtually no impression on him as a collectivist economy; for nearly all of his references to communism or Marxism are concerned with "illusions" in Marxist theory or with the moral perversion displayed in Russian politics. It would appear that he is somewhat like the Roman historian who could no longer bear the ills of the present nor any remedies for them.

A final glance at *The Children of Light and the Children of Darkness* will indicate what is meant. Here the theologian has lost virtually all devotion to Marxian perspectives and strategies, despite the remark that "A theory emphasizing the social character of industrial property is closer to the truth than the bourgeois creed which insists on its individual character." * He scores the Marxian ideas

---

* In discussing the question of a new name to replace the title of the journal, *Radical Religion* in the Winter issue, (1940) Niebuhr writes: "We are socialists in the field of politics in that we believe that the socialization of property is a basic condition of health in a technical society." But he says no more here about

of property as the root of all evil, of human nature as good, of government as "the executive committee of the possessing classes," of a coming utopia beyond the Revolution. He is now fearful of coercion and potential dictatorship, being suspicious even of the ultimate effects of "democratic" socialization, since a socialization of "large-scale industrial property" might issue in a control by "economic managers" over the whole range of economic and political institutions (p. 113). He acknowledges that none of his "propositions solves any specific issue of property in a given instance," for after all "democracy is a method of finding proximate solutions for insoluble problems" (p. 118). Though he does not say so directly, what he really offers is a general intellectual scheme from a Christian perspective; but such a scheme is not exactly a political and economic theory.*

Since Niebuhr therefore rejects orthodox Marxism for all its insights; and since the bourgeois politics of Democratic and Republican parties does not appeal to him; and since he is rather disillusioned with American "doctrinaire" socialism, it appears that no alternative is left save for a strategy difficult to distinguish from a virtual political reformism.† Perhaps he cannot sanction existing forms of socialism because none of them offers an encouraging promise for the

socialism save that he immediately launches into a repetition of his familiar tirades against Marxist illusions.

* One must admit that the development of a significant intellectual framework making a serious use of historic Christian perspectives is a major achievement, particularly in a country like the United States where the viewpoint of naturalistic philosophy and empirical science has attained such a tremendous vogue throughout the academic world. But the brilliance of this creative endeavor need not entice us into the assumption that a theory of human nature and a philosophy of history can render unnecessary the construction of a politico-economic theory relevant to the struggle for justice in our generation.

† Illustrative of Niebuhr's cautious, pragmatic politics is his distrust of proposals for world government, his confidence being placed primarily in the quest for a new balance of power between Russia and the United States. Likewise discussion of suggestions for a new political alignment (reported in the New York daily, PM, November 12, 1944) brought from him little faith in the possibilities of a third party. He recommended only a "national organization of progressives" to defeat the probable coalition of various reactionary groups. "Let history," he said, "determine whether or not this will result in a third party."

days immediately ahead. Again, his major distrust of current schemes may be that they are all too secularistic, too much tempted by irresponsible power, with the result that a truly realistic Christianity cannot take the risk of identifying itself again with potentially corrupting forces. Certainly these human programs, involving a fight for power and prestige, are all perennially beset by sinful pretensions. Possibly all these considerations play a part in the rather unique phenomenon of a Christian revolutionary who leads a Fellowship of *Socialist* Christians disavowing any and all forms of doctrinaire socialism.

To many political rebels and Christian zealots alike such an outlook appears to be permeated with an enervating pessimism. A careful study of Niebuhr's total approach, however, reveals a strange brand of social pessimism. It involves merely a gloomy reaction to events, programs and ideas when they are regarded as symbols of a coming utopia or as expressions of unqualified justice. Even socialism, Marxist or Revisionist, borne on the wings of an unreserved optimism meets his sharp disapproval. On the other hand his "pessimism" is set within a striking context of attitudes, moods and perspectives which result in an enthusiastic championing of causes or a hailing of events which challenge the status quo. Consequently, events may be highly significant as symbols of change in a struggle for righteousness and as expressions of the Cosmic Purpose moving in a mysterious way toward ultimate, supra-historical fulfillment. Such a position is neither pessimism nor optimism in the ordinary sense of these words, but a special type of theological, dialectical realism.

8

Neo-Protestantism vs. Social Gospel Idealism

1. *General Character of Neo-Protestant Thought*

MODERN PROTESTANT thought in America, that is, the most recent trend in such thought, has been characterized variously as Neo-orthodoxy, Theology of Crisis, Neo-Protestantism, "dialectical" theology, the "new supernaturalism," "realism," "Neo-conservative" Christianity. In varying degrees it regards itself as a repudiation or a profound modification of the Weltanschauung of nineteenth-century Christian liberalism. It is difficult to pigeon-hole the kind of thinking referred to because on the one hand no word or phrase is likely to catch the full meaning of this intellectual-religious impulse, and on the other all sorts of thinkers are involved, some of whom confidently attack liberalism while others just as confidently preserve it—with modifications. Two of the chief American exponents of this Christian realistic emphasis, Professors Reinhold Niebuhr and John C. Bennett of the Union Theological Seminary, symbolize the difficulty of hard-and-fast delineation. The former is a severe critic of bourgeois Christianity, liberalism, social reformism, Kingdom of God utopianism, illusory and optimistic modernism, accepting frankly the responsibility of promoting a revolt against such superficial religion and culture. The latter, who works in closest collaboration with Dr. Niebuhr, shares this rebellious spirit but considers himself

[131]

one who has simply helped to bring liberalism into a more vital connection with modern issues.

All sorts of influences have helped to shape this new religious spirit—European theology, particularly that of Barth and Brunner, a rediscovery of hitherto obscured values in historic Christianity, revival of the ideas of Paul, Augustine, Luther and Kierkegaard, world-wide trend toward a more fundamental church loyalty, and cultural factors like the growth of secularism, humanism and Marxism. Negative forces of importance are breakdown in plans for social transformation, disappointment over proletarian revolution, degradation of ecclesiastical institutions, the threat of fascism, and the virtual wreckage of so-called Christian civilization through all manner of confusions and worldly aspirations, most notably of all through global wars followed by unstable peace arrangements. We do not essay here to point out elements of cause and effect, which is virtually impossible anyway, save in a tentative and highly unsatisfactory fashion. All that can be noted is that such factors as listed, together with many, many others, are important aspects of a total world situation which forms the setting for this pronounced theological revolt.

There is some justification for using each and all of the terms indicated above for describing the ideas under consideration. This is "neo-orthodoxy" because it is a return to a more conservative, more "orthodox" or "dogmatic" position in comparison with the dominant trends of the last two generations. In no sense, however, is it a revival of the orthodoxy of Catholicism, Anglicanism, Lutheranism or American Protestant Fundamentalism of the Baptist, Methodist and Presbyterian types. It is just as much a protest against these historic orthodoxies as it is against liberal Christianity, although it endeavors to preserve values in both. Since it is for the most part a Protestant movement, almost entirely so in the United States, it has been aptly called a Neo-Protestantism.* But such thinking is also "dialectical." As noted in the preceding chapter, this word is employed by the theologian today not in the original Socratic sense as being "conversational" or "argumentative," but in a special sig-

* Europe has not only a strong Neo-orthodoxy in Protestantism but also in Eastern or "Greek" Catholicism. In Britain Anglicanism is likewise deeply influenced by the recent trends.

nification as a type of logical (or rational) process which seeks to achieve truth and reality by focusing attention on the tension between opposite but equally valid truths. Throughout this whole movement one finds a sustained effort to avoid extremes, to escape the embarrassment of one-sided emphasis on special doctrines, values and loyalties. There is a quest for a total view, a wholeness, a "polarity," a fusion of the most contradictory aspects of reality. If "realism" is the expression which is most frequently used, it is not because it is actually more descriptive than others, but possibly because it is less offensive to the American temper. We Americans like to think of ourselves as stern, practical, tough-minded, rooted in the hard facts of life and experience. Besides, terms like "dialectical," "Continental," "Barthian" are too European! Ours must be an indigenous movement, as in truth it is, although perhaps more profoundly influenced by European ideas and experiences than many are inclined to acknowledge. Nonetheless the term realism is as good as any; for it serves at least to indicate that such religious thought desires to face squarely and honestly the realities (however unpleasant) of our cultural and religious situation.

There are numerous works which reveal the fundamental character of this type of thinking. One of the earliest is by Niebuhr, Pauck and Miller, *The Church Against the World*.[1] Other books describing it are E. E. Aubrey, *Present Theological Tendencies* (1936), W. M. Horton, *Realistic Theology* (1934) and *Contemporary Continental Theology* (1938), C. C. Morrison, *What is Christianity?* (1940), John C. Bennett, *Christian Realism* (1941) and *Christian Ethics and Social Policy* (1946), and Charles D. Kean, *Christianity and the Cultural Crisis* (1945). The literary products which deserve special attention as being classic formulations of this Neo-orthodoxy or "Christian realism" are the aforementioned writings coming from the pen of Reinhold Niebuhr.* Likewise the works of Paul J. Tillich of the Union Theological Seminary belong in this category.[2] Kean's *Christianity and the Cultural Crisis* and Bennett's *Christian Ethics*

---

* We have seen that Niebuhr's first explosive volume appeared in 1932, entitled *Moral Man and Immoral Society*. Since then, aside from numerous articles, a stream of books has poured forth expressing in vigorous style and profuse argument the anti-liberal viewpoint.

and Social Policy both set forth an excellent, constructive, well-rounded presentation of the essential point of view as it bears upon concrete social problems.[3]

This whole trend in the direction of theological reconstruction expresses itself in disillusionment and in revolt. It is revolt against autonomous reason, which was too individualistic, too negative, too pretentious, too humanistic (man-centered), too anti-church and anti-theological, too unrealistic about human nature and human institutions. Pointing out the fateful intellectual step taken at the opening of our modern era, Professor Tillich charges: "Here belief in autonomous reason declared and justified itself to the mind of man. Reason was conceived as the organ of truth, in philosophy as well as in science, in the humanities as well as in psychology and sociology." The dire practical consequences are now in evidence. "The quest for truth became a method of foreseeing the future instead of creating it. Rational truth was replaced by instincts and pragmatic beliefs. And the instincts and beliefs were those of the ruling classes and their conventions. Philosophy was largely restricted to epistemology.[4] Reinhold Niebuhr contends that idealists identify "spirit too simply with reason," while romanticists emphasize too much either "natural vitality" or "natural unities and forms as sources of order and virtue." Thus the human spirit in its pride "claims unconditioned validity for its systems of logical coherence and rational unities."[5] Kean does not use the phrase "autonomous reason," but his argument is in the same vein. He attacks scientific method, the "cult of objectivity," the presumptuous empiricist theory of a "continuous universe" and of "autonomous and impersonal" social laws and forces.[6]

The denunciation of autonomous reason is but the other side of a positive demand for commitment, decision, "existential" thinking. Dr. Tillich describes the nature of this "existential" (or "critical," "decisional") approach as one which "concerns us as living, deciding men." The truth involved "has a character quite different from the truth of reason, whether humanistic reason or technical reason," for it "cannot be gained by detached analysis and verifiable hypothesis." While he believes in the necessity for achieving a more inclusive "rational truth," he still contends that if "existential truth with its practical bearing on religious and ethical activity is excluded, Christian faith becomes relativistic and sterile." [7] Kean declares that we cannot "arrogate to ourselves a specious disinterestedness in the events of history. They are not external. We are part of them. We are involved in them." [8]

The underlying assumption of these theological rebels is that there is after all no such thing as genuine, absolute disinterestedness or objectivity. Champions of agnostic empiricism or humanistic naturalism possess only, in the language of Kean, "a cult of objectivity." A thinker like David Hume proved over two centuries ago that the basic concepts of science cannot be demonstrated beyond doubt to correspond to objective reality. In our day A. N. Whitehead has contended that the whole of modern science is erected on the dogma of an "order of nature" unprovable in the metaphysical sense. Hence a higher "reason" in man, a kind of profound religious and moral logic, justifies one in a faith in the validity of decision. Those who draw other conclusions are not thereby inherently more objective merely because they rest comfortably in the delusion of a pseudo-objectivity clothed in the phraseology of scientific empiricism.

But the concept of crisis applies to society, civilization, in fact to the whole of history. The Neo-orthodox charge rationalistic liberalism with an essentially rosy view of human existence, a view which looks upon social crisis as an occasional, accidental, temporary, surface phenomenon. The illusion of modern man is focused at this point. It is based upon a perspective which fails to penetrate the ugly tragic nature of historical reality. Modernists, trusting in temporarily constructed systems of security, overlook the brutality of both history and nature, fail to see the inevitable doom of all earthly would-be paradises, misconstrue every outburst of disorder which shatters their flimsily built structures. Lacking the profundity of the Christian perspective we trust that progress is really inherent in human existence, and that each disturbance, even of total war, is but an essentially surface event which reveals that human institutions are still somewhat maladjusted, are as yet characterized by "cultural lag." Niebuhr thus proclaims that modern utopianism, primarily a heritage of the Renaissance credo of progress, has an "optimistic attitude towards the whole historical process." This Renaissance world-view "believed that the cumulations of knowledge and the extensions of reason, the progressive conquest of nature . . . the technical extension of social cohesion, all of which inhere in the 'progress' of history, were guarantees of the gradual conquest of chaos and evil by the force of reason and order." [9] Tillich maintains that "the Christian message cannot anticipate a future situation devoid of tragedy even if the demonic forces in the present situation be conquered. The authentic Christian message is never utopian whether through belief in progress or through faith in revolution." [10]

The assault of the theological radicals is directed also against secularism in all its forms. Such secularism has been a growing cancer in modern society, the Neo-orthodox maintain. It has appeared in the form of a superficial, dogmatic lack of appreciation of our spiritual heritage, particularly of the heritage of Christian thought. Even Christianity in its liberal form had been infected by an increasingly humanistic emphasis, becoming at times anti-church and anti-theological in spirit. The social gospel idealism was often an undisciplined passion for social reform, a passion grounded neither in an understanding of the depths of theology nor in a genuine loyalty to the Christian church and Christian traditions. It frequently spent its energies in tirades against Scriptural ideas, in scorn of systematic formulations of doctrinal truth, in indifference toward worship, and in reckless experiments in religious education which was neither religious nor educating in any significantly Christian meaning of the term. Science had become such an obsession, such a messiah, that religious zealots often were much less concerned about the propagation of the faith than they were in defending an empiricism born and nurtured in the bosom of naturalism.

Hence the assault upon the dominant forms of Christianity itself. Such religion had adjusted itself within the framework of a culture which was alien to its highest hopes and deepest desires. The more orthodox types had lost their relevance to the social and intellectual needs of an era which could no longer understand even the language employed. Such Christianity entrenched itself behind dogmas, creeds, ecclesiastical traditions and forms of worship which nevertheless could not conceal its aloofness, conceit and irresponsibility in regard to a lost generation. It usually proclaimed in sonorous phrases its devotion to the Kingdom of God while growing fat upon the contributions offered by the kingdoms of this world. Even its education was incredibly barren, as it never gave up (in Protestant circles at least) the naive idea that evangelistic appeals were ultimately and finally sufficient for all "spiritual" and social needs. As for "progressive" religion, it too was equally "adjusted." Its preoccupation was with scientific theology, non-committal sociology, and agnostic educational techniques which strengthened the delusion that men, even religious men, could emancipate themselves from all dogmas. Such "liberal" Christianity was continually leading its devotees to the precipice of humanism and naturalism, with a result that religion itself became no longer a quest for truth but a passion for personal growth and self-expression. The upshot is that modernized Christianity, which on its practical side was the social gospel, was committed to an interpretation of life and an adaptation to modern culture, which not merely allowed it to support autonomous reason, scientific tentativeness, naturalism and secularism but even to identify these with Christianity itself.

Outside of professional religious circles secularism marched on in boldness in every area—in art, belles lettres, education, science, politics, business, philosophy. Speaking of the nineteenth century, Professor Tillich affirms that the "gargantuan mechanism of an industrial civilization was swelling to the height of its power and bringing every aspect of thought as well as life under its sway, thus radically transforming the guiding principles of the human mind as well as the actual conditions of human existence." He continues by charging that "the spirit of the times became skeptical, positivistic and conservative in every respect with the single exception of technical science." Moreover, the "natural sciences furnished the pattern for all knowledge, and also for practical life and religion.[11] Such secularism sometimes clothed itself philosophically in the quiet humanism of a John Dewey or of an M. C. Otto; at other times in atheistic defiance like that of Bertrand Russell's *A Free Man's Worship*. With most people, however, professional or lay, it appeared as an undisturbed, half-cynical indifference to religion and the church as if such matters were trivial and inconsequential to their existence. For the most part the Christian cause was not directly attacked, but simply ignored.

While on its intellectual side Neo-Protestantism manifests its spirit in defiance of secularism and naturalism in all their varieties, on its practical side it challenges uncritical alliance with secular political parties and social reform movements. Such parties and movements make at least three perennial errors, it is argued. First they act upon assumptions which place too great confidence in human nature; that is, they oversimplify the motives of men. They take for granted the purity of their own aspirations, the unqualified rightness of their causes, while ascribing to their enemies pure evil and injustice. For such devotees of uncompromising social strategy each struggle is likely to be interpreted as one between White and Black, between the Saints and the Demons. Profound religion knows this to be an oversimplification. In the second place these secular parties by their very zeal, fanaticism and blind force, generated in virtually all class conflicts, tend to aggravate the total human situation. They often add to the divisions, the cliques, the narrow parties and self-centered groups which already over-burden the race of men. In their passion they not infrequently engender hatreds, cruelties and all manner of sins committed not seldom in the name of justice. In the third place, their hopes are usually extravagant and utopian, lacking the depth of understanding which knows that the fiery revolutionary dreams of today become the empty, burned out creeds of tomorrow.

The Christianity which is now disintegrating, it is charged, had vitiated itself by endorsement of an alliance with just such narrow, conceited, short-sighted, fanatical programs, movements and parties. It put its faith in Prohibitionism, Socialism, Single-taxism, trade unionism, democracy, Marxism, New Dealism, and other one-sided programs. We are leaving behind a fantastic era, it is said, in which social gospel idealism was actually fed upon the delusive hopes that in a generation or so the Kingdom of God itself would be erected upon the sands of time, first perhaps in the United States, the citadel of capitalist culture!

While it is possibly too early to assess accurately the positive doctrinal elements in this intellectual and spiritual fermentation, the general directions are in evidence. There is a tendency to restore theological doctrine, worship and church loyalty to a position of primacy in the thought and action of believers. The insights of the great Christian minds of the past are appropriated with a desire to gain their views of man, his nature, plight, possibilities and destiny.

Moreover, discussions of doctrine and church have taken a decidedly supernaturalistic, absolutistic turn. Many of the foremost thinkers, particularly Tillich and Reinhold Niebuhr, proclaim principles, doctrines and perspectives which transcend nature, reason and history. The former declares in *The Interpretation of History* (1936) that "history itself cannot overcome itself and its supporting powers. Only through the appearance of a super-historical unconditioned meaning can history gain an ultimate foundation" (pp. 260–261). The latter accepts "prophetic Messianism" which, while not denying the meaning of history and life, nevertheless affirms that such meanings "can be understood only in terms of a dimension deeper and higher than the system of nature," and that "there are obscurities and contradictions in the 'behaviour' of history which can be clarified only if the unique purpose of God is more fully disclosed." [12] Even in regard to humanity, he asserts that "the second important characteristic of the Christian view of man is that he is understood primarily from the standpoint of relation to nature. He is made in the 'image of God.'" [13]

The religious community has acquired new meaning, receiving a central place in such thinking. Corporate worship gains a fresh emphasis. The Christian church, fellowship or movement is not merely an object of praise, loyalty, emotional attachment, spiritual retreat. It is sometimes interpreted, as with C. C. Morrison,[14] in a quasi-Catholic fashion, as if it were itself the revelation on earth of a special, unique and even supernatural institution. Indeed, it is when dealing with the "sustaining community," as well as with the great doctrines of God, Christ, sin and salvation, that Neo-orthodoxy speaks in language reminiscent of the supernaturalism of past generations. But restoration of the church to a foremost place has another special significance. It tends to provide a base and a center of reference for social action. Social action is now usually regarded as having been largely undisciplined, uncoordinated, and unchecked in the preceding half century or more when the social gospel idealism reigned. Again, the "ecumenical" or world church is an important trend, receiving more and more emphasis as a result of the war crisis. Outstanding churchmen like H. P. Van Dusen, John Bennett, John A. Mackay, H. S. Leiper and C. S. Macfarland are enthusiastic spokesmen for this cause.[15]

2. *The Social Gospel Viewpoint Restated*

In considering a complex, many-faceted impulse like the social gospel there are two approaches which must be guarded against. One is the temptation to reduce the phenomenon, whether on the side of its ideology or of its social program, to a more or less consistent pattern. As we have seen this reformist spirit manifested itself in varying degrees and patterns ranging from a fairly conservative social science research to revolutionary political thought and action. Even today we can see social gospel spokesmen as far apart politically as are Harry F. Ward and the late Charles A. Ellwood. Care must be taken also to avoid treating this general type of thought, whether before or after 1900, as if it were equivalent to a religious humanism. Such a tendency appeared of course in the twenties, but even then out-and-out humanism was a minor feature of Christian liberalism.

An opposite temptation is to minimize the peculiar character of social gospel Christianity by treating it as if it represented merely a general social optimism or Christian social action temporarily tainted with an element of utopianism. Rather is the social gospel here interpreted as a phase of a certain fairly distinctive type of religion— American liberal Christianity. It is the application to society of certain fundamental principles and perspectives which grow out of definite theological, philosophical and social views. Hutchison made a suggestive observation when he noted, in regard to the Federal Council's outlook, that here "is a body of social thought" which "approaches the status of a significant social philosophy," and which differs from "other historic Christian social philosophies." [16]

Visser 't Hooft perceived this uniqueness in liberalized, socialized American religion, suggesting that it was "an application of Christian ideals in a novel way," introducing "new elements into all departments of Christian thought." It was, he declared, not merely an application of Christian principles to society, but "an application of social principles to Christianity" as well.[17] In short, our assumption is that social gospel Christianity is the practical aspect of a unique type of religion with both a special doctrinal coloring—that is, a distinctive theological outlook—and a marked pattern of social thought and action which ties in with the theology. Despite the fact that there is neither strict inner consistency nor linear historical growth, the dominant traits and tendencies of such social Christianity can be seen.

A central feature of such religion was strong belief in the inherent ethical, religious and intellectual capacity of man. While men were regarded as "sinners" who were self-seeking, ignorant, blind, weak, and standing in need of redemption, as a matter of fact this was a minor note. The emphasis was placed on the goodness of human nature, on the tremendous moral and spiritual possibilities in creatures made in the image of God. Jesus was usually presented as the Supreme Example, as the Great Teacher, as the "Savior" who redeemed men basically by showing to them the saving grace which comes through walking in the "way of the Cross." True, God was needed, but equally important—indeed, of paramount importance —was the fact that man can cooperate with God. Together the divine and human labor for the reign of righteousness, but without human effort, devotion, and self-sacrifice, no kingdom on earth is possible! If men but learn the lofty truths found in the simple gospel of the Master, in the "social principles" of New Testament religion, they will find themselves becoming progressively more charitable, cooperative, tolerant, kindly-disposed, democratic. Social justice, civilized progress, the coming Kingdom—all depends upon the widespread acceptance and practice of the gospel of brotherhood. The need of the hour was for more education, more Christian organization, more deeds of charity, more evangelism, more democratic discussion, more social legislation.

The conception of God was one which majored in the creed of immanence, minored in transcendence. While traditional Calvinism tended more to combine a theological other-worldliness with an ethical this-worldliness, social gospel Christianity finally lopped off much of the super-mundane framework, leaving the supernatural element largely as a sort of theological relish making an essentially naturalized religion more palatable for the tender-minded. Rather was God seen in the beauties of nature, in the evolution of democratic government, in the profound wisdom of the philosophical mind, in the struggle for social reform, in the upthrust of the universe as it obeyed the divinely ordained cosmic laws. God was in man, in life, in society, in the universe as the inward drive in the unceasing struggle to achieve truth, beauty and goodness. Heaven was the natural realization on earth of the human dream for the Kingdom of Brotherhood. Whether the stress was on Christian sociology, religious communism, an ideal democratic commonwealth, or humanitarian social service, God was conceived as the divine power working through men and institutions to achieve the Good Society. Moreover, man and God were equally important factors in the cosmic drama.

Advocates of the social gospel exhibited a recognizable attitude toward history, society and institutional processes. They not only tended to minimize a Divine Being high above the world, but they discouraged emphasis on a Kingdom beyond the world, as well as enthusiasm for a "church against the world." Civilization was the great theater in which God fulfilled his purposes, the church being one among many agencies working out such purposes. This present existence is of superlative value—its joys, sorrows, failures, achievements, possibilities. Life is not a pilgrimage or a preparation for eternity. Rather are the natural material, social and intellectual values of the cultural life goods in themselves which the Supreme Being ordained for his children to enjoy. Ideals of asceticism, world flight, world renunciation, dreams of a celestial city beyond this place of wrath and tears, were brushed aside as either of little religious or cultural significance, or as manifestations of the outgrown childhood aberrations of the human spirit. The Christian battle is a battle to preserve, improve and enjoy the fruits of human culture built through millenniums of untold human sacrifice. Hence the social gospel was a gospel tied to faith in the Christian worth of "progressive" social institutions, organizations, movements, enterprises. A sharp distinction between the Kingdom and natural human society disappeared, for progressive society was virtually identified with the earliest phases of the gradually approaching Kingdom. The church-centered Kingdom of Catholicism, the eternal transcendent Kingdom of Augustine, the eschatological Kingdom of early Christianity—all these conceptions dropped out of this type of thought which tended to see the eternal purposes of God objectified in the unfolding of a humane social order. The gradualism and naturalism of historical processes replaced apocalypticism, eschatology, and emphasis upon supra-historical realities.

Thus we see a concentration on institutional progress and social reconstruction as contrasted with concern for individual salvation on the one hand and ecclesiastical systems on the other. The title of an influential book of lectures published by Canon Fremantle in 1885 expresses the viewpoint perfectly: *The World is the Object of Redemption*. Fremantle here declared: "The main object of effort is not to be found either in the saving of individual souls out of a ruined world; or in the organization of a separate society destined always to be held aloof from the world, but in the saving of the world itself." When the *Brotherhood of the Commonwealth* was launched in 1896 it came forth with the avowed aim of establishing "Mutualism or the Kingdom of God Here and Now." Bellamy's "Nationalism" was heralded widely as the visible appearance of God's new order. *The Dawn,* official organ of the Society of Christian Socialists, affirmed in 1890 that the "aim of Socialism is embraced in the aim of Christianity." *The Kingdom,* edited by H. W. Gleason, made the challenging claim that the "social question, the industrial problem, the race problem, the questions of international relations—in fact every question involved in the relation of man to man—must be brought into the School of Christ and answered there" (issue of May, 1898). H. D. Lloyd went so far as to denounce the church in wholesale fashion in 1906, publishing a work entitled *Man the Social Creator* in which he lyrically exclaimed: "All the beauties and helps of the old-fashioned trust in God will some day re-appear in a trust in man"; for humanity is the "representation of God." The church, he argued, is co-extensive with all mankind. Even Walter Rauschenbusch maintained that "religious belief in the Fatherhood of God, in the fraternal solidity of men, and in the ultimate social redemption of the race through Christ lends a religious quality to Socialist ideals." *

In the post-1900 social gospel period, although utopian socialism and revolutionary fervor tended to drop into the background, the emphasis on social change was just as great. As we have noted, a fever for application of the "principles of Jesus" to society broke out among the ecclesiastical bodies. Social service commissions, councils and leagues became common. The famous "Social Creed" which was adopted by the Federal Council of Churches in 1908 was quickly thereafter adopted by most of the leading denominations, at least a dozen such denominational groups launching upon social service programs. The "Men and Religion Forward Movement" but echoed the mood of the era when it accepted as its task the "permanent enlistment [of men and boys] in the program of Jesus Christ as the world program of daily affairs." Referring to the Federal Council's "Creeds" of 1908 and 1932, John A. Hutchison remarks that "the general attitude or spirit of liberal reformism, midway between standpat conservatism and revolutionary radicalism, seeking to remold existing human forms and institutions into something nearer the Kingdom of God underlies both creeds." [18]

The position of social gospel Christianity in regard to theological doctrine in general, and to Jesus and the Church in particular, is too well known to require rehearsal here.[19] Suffice it to say that such religion possessed besides its vague hope of social progress, at least four other great dogmas, or rather slogans: social justice, brotherhood, the "social principles" of Jesus as the heart of religion, and the Kingdom of God on earth as the goal of history. The ethical and the social thus were regarded as of paramount importance, the theological as secondary. Indeed, ethical, political and economic principles were sometimes identified with the essence of Christianity. At times this position would go to the length of contending, as did Ely, that Jesus' commandment of love "when elaborated becomes social

---

* Article on "Christian Socialism" in a *Dictionary of Religion and Ethics,* edited by Mathews and Smith, pp. 90–91. Rauschenbusch is not only regarded usually as the best representative of the social gospel, but he is perhaps the most balanced of its exponents. He nevertheless shares most of the emphases and perspectives found in early twentieth-century progressive Christianity.

science or sociology." Or with Herron it might call revolutions "even in their wildest forms" the "impulses of God." With Professor A. W. Small it could hail Jesus as "after all, the profoundest economist"; or call the Bible a book of "political economy" in which "God's laws of property" are written, as did *Equity,* organ of the Christian Labor Union. In most cases such extreme views were not advocated, but the prevailing temper was to think of social and ethical values as the full content of that which was significant in the Christian religion.

Today this social gospel viewpoint is displayed in the thinking of considerable numbers of American Christians, among whom men like E. Stanley Jones, Ellwood, McConnell, Page and Ward are but a few outstanding examples. Indeed, this position is doubtless as yet the prevailing outlook in educated religious circles, ecclesiastical and lay. There may be pronounced variations in specific beliefs or in specific attitudes toward innumerable social problems. Then too the purely theological may move toward the vanishing point, as was the case in the thought of Ellwood and Ward; or it may assume a large place in the thinker's range of interests, as with McConnell. The emphasis might be on worship and evangelism, as is true of both Jones and Page. Or, as again with Page (or Ward) the consuming interest may turn to radical politics. But whatever the particular line of attack or whatever the area of more or less professional responsibility, the social gospel spokesmen usually seek primarily to accommodate religion to mundane affairs by discouraging emphasis on theology and speculation, by urging adoption of science and progressive education, advocating the employment of Christianity as a means of reform, and by proclaiming the ideal society dawning on earth. Religion to them is first and foremost an instrument of cultural change. All else is secondary to this central function, even when personal redemption is taken into account.

3. *Neo-Protestantism's Attack on Social Gospel Idealism*

In the light of our definition of the social gospel Neo-Protestantism constitutes a challenge to it. This historic movement in America, as has been indicated, is to be identified not with religious-social idealism as such nor with Christian social action in general. And it is more than a "sense of the social responsibility of the church." The social gospel was a gospel of progress, of extreme faith in the fundamental virtue and rationality of men, of hope in the speedy transformation of social institutions in the direction of the Good Society. Again, it was a movement which would subordinate theology as such—or even the church—to the great task of social reconstruction. Its theological orientation, its philosophy of man and society, as well as its conception of the coming Kingdom on earth, thus was inseparable from its political hopes and strategies.

The validity of the contention here is further confirmed by the fact that Neo-orthodoxy centers its criticism on this religious idealism in both its theological and political aspects. The following theological presuppositions, all challenged by the Neo-Protestant perspective, are more or less characteristic of social gospel thinking:

1. That the Bible, particularly Jesus or his teaching, is primarily concerned about the regulation or rebuilding of social institutions and relationships in this present world.
2. That the ultimate problems of human destiny—theological or metaphysical problems—are secondary as compared with the reconstruction of civilization or a given society.
3. That in fact serious and sustained preoccupation with these ultimate "theological" issues tends to destroy or at least to weaken the passion for the solution of immediate, most urgent human problems.
4. That religion after all is mainly an agency for civilized progress, a means or technique (among others) for revolutionizing society; it is not to the same extent a gateway to salvation in a supernatural, suprahistorical world. *
5. That contemporary society is already in process of transformation, and the central challenge to Christianity is to join other forces demanding still further transformation.
6. That the purpose of God is to build with human aid an ideal society on earth—a society which appropriately may be called the Kingdom of God.

* It is important to note that the contrast here is not between the personal and social, nor between "devotional" and "social" religion. Obviously many social gospel thinkers give a large place to the personal and devotional. The principal contrast here is between the natural and supernatural, or between the historical and supra-historical.

Concerning the outlook implied in these six condensed statements one can discern a tendency to focus attention on religion as an instrument of social change, with a minimum of concern for theological matters. And there is no absorption in an absolutist, suprahistorical Kingdom, nor in a transcendent church regarded as basically alien to mundane affairs. On the contrary, the central preoccupation is with social events taking place in the realm of the Here and Now. The primary importance of Christianity is the part which it plays in furthering changes in our environment. Thus whether it be concerned with an academic sociology, an energetic, courageous political reformism, a socialism of the radical Marxist or parliamentary type, a utopian Kingdom of God, a democratic utopia, or with "progressive" preaching, journalism and social service, the social gospel idealism apparently did not take eternity very seriously. For such an outlook was absorbed mainly, almost exclusively, with the glorious prospects of a human utopia erected on the sands of time.

Neo-Protestantism demands a fresh orientation and a new emphasis, as we have seen. But the attack is not merely upon this theological perspective; it is equally upon any "unrealistic" orientation toward the political problem. Hence the Neo-orthodox would make the following charges against the social gospel's approach to politics:

1. That it possesses a superficial, too simple, too rationalistic conception of essential human nature, particularly as human nature shows itself in political activity and organization.
2. That it often holds an exaggerated confidence in the possibilities of fundamental social change, of ecclesiastical, economic or political reconstruction.
3. That its over-optimism about social processes and institutions leads frequently to dangerous, and at times disastrous, political predictions.
4. That it tends to identify the Christian hope of redemption too closely with specific programs and plans for social betterment.
5. That at times it unconsciously or unwittingly endorses status quo political, legal and economic structures by accepting and magnifying peripheral reforms.
6. That it sometimes pursues the illusory notion that some political formula, key idea, or some striking social scheme can bring a general solution for humanity's woes thus leading rapidly to a paradise on earth.
7. That it fails to preserve adequately the healthy tension which ought

to obtain between ultimate religious norms and the various transitory secularistic ideals and movements in a given society.

8. That by its recurrent moods of exaggerated optimism and pessimism it shows itself lacking in important resources for facing the ugly tragic realities involved in social crises and incident to thoroughgoing cultural reconstruction.

9. That it has under-rated or at least thrown out of proper focus the central necessity of the church as an agency of control in the realm of Christian social thought and action.

What the Neo-orthodox seek consequently is not the destruction of social action as such, but of the social gospel's exaggerated political optimism and its theological superficiality. The present world situation, together with a fresh study of human history, has convinced the "realists" that those who pin their hopes unqualifiedly either in present trends toward social rebuilding or in a distant ideal society among men are destined to see their faith suffering disillusionment, not to say catastrophic disturbances. The argument goes further, even to the point of challenging the prevailing interpretation of the nature of Christianity. To these Neo-Protestants the essence of all profound religion is that it views the supernatural order as a pressing reality. They feel that one pathetic blunder of the past generation of reformist Christians in America was the temptation virtually to naturalize Jesus and the Bible, when even the most unsophisticated intellect can perceive immediately upon entering the world of the New Testament that here is no concern in the least for an ideal civilization or for a "Christian culture." The very essence of the message of Jesus is the proclamation, as even Harnack the arch-liberal once wrote, of "eternal life in the midst of time." A mentality immersed completely in the immediate values of social systems, though it may make genuinely reverent bows in the direction of a transcendental reality, cannot escape the temptation to give hostages to secularism and to treat its faith as if it were a mere tool for short-range purposes.

4. Neo-Protestant Approach to the Current Social Crisis

Some readers holding in mind the title of our volume referring to "social idealism" may wonder about this apparently disproportionate emphasis upon the *theological* aspects of Protestant realism. There are several important reasons for this emphasis. In the first place, the movement is through and through theological. It consciously envisages a restoration of the pristine glory of theology. It is first and foremost a *theological* revolt, an emphatic intellectual-spiritual protest against a scientific, naturalistic theology or religious philosophy. It desires to make theology itself more deeply and truly "Christian," more firmly rooted in the great dogmas, insights, meanings and points of view which have come down through the ecclesiastical and biblical traditions. Equally important is the fact that it is a *theological critique* of man, society and culture rather than a scientific, philosophical or sociological critique.* It aims at bringing the central Christian theories, affirmations, and "saving" truths to bear upon the world situation. Indeed, the feeling is widespread in religious circles that *only* these "saving" truths, hitherto ignored or scorned by modern man, can relieve the dilemma and tragedy of human life. Hence, Neo-Protestantism possesses its own distinctive approach to the analysis of the depression, the war, the frustrated hopes of peace, the menace of the machine, the mounting conflicts among races, classes, and nations. In this diagnosis is revealed the peculiar character of this type of thought in its attitude toward society, social processes, reforms and revolutions, economic and political institutions, and toward social strategies.

Aside from the recent appearance of the atom bomb, four major cataclysmic events have exploded in our world since the War of 1914–18. They were the Russian Revolution, the world depression, the appearance of fascism, and the outbreak of a new global war. All these events, whether viewed as causes or symbols, were certainly forces which could not be ignored or treated casually by any race, nation or social group on the face of the earth. Our social order since 1914 has been disturbed by recurrent shocks apparently of

* There may be some objection to this manner of stating the issue. Exponents of "realism" or Neo-orthodoxy would not regard their analysis as "unscientific" or "unphilosophical" in the sense of doing violence to the contributions of science and philosophy. However, in so far as so-called science and philosophy have become largely identified with tentative, non-committal, agnostic, humanistic fact-finding techniques, their point of view would be a rejection of such "naturalism." Neo-orthodoxy is committed in a somewhat a priori fashion to a supernaturalistic, theocentric outlook on the world of nature and society.

[149]

cosmic proportions. The upsetting conditions have demanded an explanation which goes beneath and beyond the usual explanations of secularistic thinkers.

American Neo-Protestantism claims that the conventional analyses are one-sided, oversimplified, superficial or inadequate. Only a profoundly "Christian" interpretation will suffice. Realistic religion thus has a *theological* view, an outlook based upon a deep understanding of both the individual and society in their relation to nature, history, and God. We are called upon, it is argued, to see society in terms of cosmic meanings, as well as to see man in the full "dimensions of his spirit." Historical events must be judged in the light of ultimate moral and spiritual principles and processes, in terms of revelation, sin, laws of love and justice, the meaning of Christ and of divine purposes. Hence, the crisis is at its roots "spiritual," not merely technological, educational, economic or political. Whether we look at communism or fascism, world depression or world wars, international anarchy or domestic class conflict, the underlying factors are the same.

In a more or less sweeping fashion let us look at some of the major constructive contributions of American Protestant realism. Very significant is the demand for radical intellectual and spiritual reorientation. There is scarcely room for doubt, on the part of those seeking a profound understanding of the chaos of modern social life, that no way out of our paralysis is possible without a frank facing of the results of traditional rationalistic, secularistic, egocentric views of human life. Whether a reconstruction of civilization is possible or not, the demonstration of the inadequacy of the individualistic-secularistic perspective is convincing. Pagan rationalism—that is, a rationalism which ignores the historic Christian pessimism about the "natural man"—simply does not grasp the depths of evil in personal or collective human nature. When life is running with a surface smoothness, such a mentality tends to rest comfortably in the delight and pursuits of natural goods, often entertaining hopes for a continued smoothness or easy restoration when a balance is upset. In periods or situations when social structures are in total disintegration, the pagan mind is baffled. It is tempted to turn either to unqualified despair, or to light-hearted irresponsible isolation from social struggle, or to cynicism in regard to all human ideals. If the temper of the secularist is an inherently optimistic one, he may deceive himself by repeated utopian expectations, never reconciling himself to the folly and perversion of human plans and programs, particularly those dearest to him. Here too was an important weakness in social gospel idealism: it likewise possessed a romantic conception of human nature, of society, of its processes and goals. The Neo-orthodox thus have shown us that whether we acknowledge man to be a sinner or not, there is certainly something in him which can be described appropriately as "demonic." There is a persistent blindness, viciousness, pride and pretension running through all human aspirations. And perhaps the most pathetic element of all in man's character is his equally stubborn refusal to admit that such ignorance, brutality, self-centeredness is deeply engrained within his being.

This re-orientation about man as a creature of nature must be extended to collective human enterprises, to social institutions, and even to civilizations. There is an inveterate tendency to regard one's own government, class, race, culture or religion as *the one criterion* for all men. In an ultimate sense collective man is always "ethnocentric," conceiving life or progress or civilization largely in terms of what has been achieved within one's own immediate sphere—usually in defiance of "outsiders" and foreign "isms." One of the most disturbing aspects of the whole effort to build an international system for the outlawry of war is the fact that American democracy and Soviet Communism each is a culture-system in which the majority of leaders are dogmatically convinced that their own petty, flimsy little structures *not only will be but ought to be* the world pattern within which all mankind will find the ideal life. Few believe seriously that our little systems have their day and will cease to be; hence we fight in fury for our temporary standards and institutions as if they were ordained by the eternal laws of the universe.

In one area the blindness about individual human weakness and about the "demonic" element in social structures comes to focus with ominous reality—in public leadership, particularly political leadership. Here men do all sorts of evil things without the slightest compunction of conscience. We make sudden and dramatic decisions about an atom bomb which may be a number one factor in causing

World War No. 3. Military and naval men behind the scenes, so to speak, employ the armed forces of a country in carrying out policies which help to destroy the potential freedom of whole races and nations. United States Senators argue and filibuster with impish glee while laying the foundation for a condition which after their deaths (if not before) may result in racial war in the country they profess to love. Business executives fight defiantly for governmental policies which if adopted would create catastrophic inflation and perhaps economic chaos. Labor bosses utilize their growing control over tens and hundreds of thousands of workers, under the imperious urge for power and social prestige, to make a political football of unions at the very hour when the future of labor is in greatest peril. All around us are men who in public capacities act in utter disregard of the indirect and ultimate effects of their attitudes, utterances, decisions and policies. The Neo-orthodox are rendering an inestimable service in trying to awaken us to the ominous fact that modern man, particularly in his collective capacities, has an easy conscience. Such a re-orientation is indispensable if we would avoid the premature doom of modern civilization. Here again is the ironical aspect of the situation—a peculiar refusal to believe seriously that doom is possible.

There is a large measure of validity in the insistence of realistic theology on interpreting our many disorders as a "cultural" crisis. True, it is embarrassing to face doctrines which underscore the notion that the very social order of which one is part is in process of radical change. It is true likewise that in a certain sense none of us can visualize in a realistic way the full, total import of this viewpoint. For it clearly implies that many of the institutions of which we are a part will be so fundamentally altered—if not destroyed—in the perhaps not-very-distant future that many of the most precious things to which we cling today will seem utterly trivial a few decades hence. There is hardly a doubt that capitalistic individualism as we know it, even in the 1940's, is in the process of rapid decay, and that the policies for which our industrialists and financiers struggle desperately will make them appear to their descendants like clowns who strutted and fretted their hours upon the stage and then were heard no more. The endeavor likewise of a nation to build a fantastically idealistic democracy upon a deeply entrenched system of social segregation and political disfranchisement of a tenth of its population must appear in the light of history as an incredible phenomenon which could excite only laughter or tears. This is not to say that utopia will dawn on some tomorrow. It is only to affirm that the acknowledgment of the fate of our social systems under the verdict of historical experience is merely to accept the assured conclusion that many aspects of our culture are having their day and already showing signs that they will cease to be.

Hence the crisis is regarded as deep-seated, radical and kaleidoscopic. It is radical because it involves a sweeping revolution in a total philosophy of life. Nothing less is demanded than the quest for a novel Christian world-view which, while doing full justice to the demands of science, industrialism and democracy, catches up the values in bourgeois culture and remolds them into a fresh system of thought neither secular nor conventionally Christian. The crisis is radical also in regard to the scope and depth of institutional transformation required. Whether through political and economic pressures or through tragically destructive conflict, most of the large institutional patterns of our time of necessity are being destroyed or reshaped into new, epoch-making configurations. While none today can predict in any direct fashion the "wave of the future" in respect to our law, politics, mores, and economic structures, or in respect to race and international relations, the forces of modern life are constantly hurling us forward, faster and faster, into unprecedented decisions, ventures, and institutional arrangements. The cultural landscape everywhere is being reshaped.

Another central and much needed message from this school of thought is the sharp emphasis upon *religious community* of a distinctively Christian type. Unfortunately both the capitalist ethos and the racist ethos are so deeply entrenched in our society that practically every would-be fellowship turns out to be a more or less continuing special interest group whose members have their primary attachments and loyalties in status quo institutions. Nonetheless, a central feature in Neo-Protestant theology is the implication of the absolute necessity for developing sooner or later such fellowships and movements as will defy all hostile institutions which are dominated by anti-Christian sentiments, traditions and doctrines —that is, "anti-Christian" as defined by the fellowships and movements themselves. It may well be that the future of American Christianity will depend upon the extent to which such tiny groups, fellowships, associations ("cells," if you please) can be created, bodies which are truly "against the world" in the sense that they find meaning and resourcefulness in the conviction of the reality and relevance of a religion transcending the narrow loyalties of class, race, and nation. At any rate, the quest for a truly Christian fellowship dominated by spiritual depth, genuine humility and social radicalism is potentially a creative outgrowth of the Neo-Protestant type of social thought. In fact, this new orientation represents an endeavor to do four necessary things: to apply the practical-ethical idealism inherited from liberal religion, to restore the theological depth of historic Christianity, to lift the church once more to a unique function in society, and to fuse these objectives into a body of principles which give Christianity both a relevance to the social struggle and a transcendence over secularism.

Notes

1

1. James Dombrowski, *The Early Days of Christian Socialism in America* (1936), p. vii (Preface).
2. Charles H. Hopkins, *The Rise of the Social Gospel in American Protestantism* (1940), p. 70.
3. *The Social Gospel Re-examined* (1940), Preface.
4. *Church and Society* (1935), p. 61.
5. See his article in *Social Action* for June 15, 1943, p. 7.
6. *Christianity and Society*, Summer, 1945, p. 11.
7. See his editorials in *The Christian Century* for March 1 and 15, 1944, under the titles respectively of "Orthodoxy, Too, Has its Social Gospel" and "Is There a Social Gospel?"
8. This meaning is given "social gospel" by Melvin J. Williams in his "Representative Sociological Contributions to Religion and Ethics," *Contemporary Social Theory* (1940), edited by Barnes and Becker. See especially pp. 866 ff.
9. The author says that we are limiting ourselves "consciously to the ideological background of the social gospel" (p. 6). Incidentally, A. C. McGiffert, Jr. has attacked Visser 't Hooft for his over-emphasis on the doctrine of an immanent, humanized God as if Rauschenbusch and his associates did not believe in a transcendent God and a transcendent Kingdom. "Walter Rauschenbusch: Twenty Years After," *Christendom*, Vol. III, No. 1 (Winter 1938).
10. *Op. cit.*, p. 21.
11. *Ibid.*, pp. 23–24. Visser 't Hooft remarks in a footnote (p. 24) that the material for his opinion is drawn largely from Chapter II of Rauschenbusch's *Christianizing the Social Order*.
12. Hopkins, *op. cit.*, p. 280.
13. Excellent and general accounts may be found in Hopkins, *op. cit.*, Chapters XVII and XVIII; F. E. Johnson, *The Social Work of the Churches* (1930); and John A. Hutchison, *We Are Not Divided* (1941). The last-named book is a doctor's dissertation subtitled "A Critical and Historical Study of the Federal Council of the Churches of Christ in America."
14. Hutchison, *We Are Not Divided*, p. 99.

2

1. *The Christ of the American Road*, pp. 48, 222, 226.
2. *Is the Kingdom of God Realism?*, pp. 55–57.

3. *Christ's Alternative to Communism* (1935), p. 168.

4. *Ibid.*, p. 199.

5. Chapters I, II, and III and VII respectively, out of a total of nine chapters, excluding the Introduction.

6. *The Christ of the American Road*, pp. 39–40.

7. This attack on Madras led to a brief controversy on the problem of the Kingdom and the church. For details see especially articles by Jones, titled respectively "Where Madras Missed the Way" and "What I Missed at Madras" in issues of *The Christian Century*, March 15 and May 31, 1939. Cf. also the article by Van Dusen in the issue of March 29, 1939: "What Stanley Jones Missed at Madras." Valuable too are letters (published April 19, 1939) written to the editor of *The Christian Century* by W. M. Horton and A. R. Ashley.

8. *Christ's Alternative to Communism*, pp. 181, 278–279.

9. *Ibid.*, p. 293.

10. *Is the Kingdom of God Realism?*, p. 18. In *The Choice Before Us* (p. 32) he speaks of the Kingdom as "the family idea operative in human affairs."

11. *The Christ of the American Road*, p. 207.

12. *Christ's Alternative to Communism*, p. 260. See also *The Christ of the American Road* (pp. 32, 129–30, 206) where he repeatedly describes "God's Order" or the Kingdom as a totalitarianism. Again, cf. *Christ's Alternative to Communism* (pp. 252 f, 254 f, 284 f) where he maintains that Christ would approve of much that is in present-day Communism.

13. *Christ's Alternative to Communism*, pp. 166, 180–181.

14. *The Christ of the American Road*, pp. 208–9. For further illustrations of the supernatural or transcendent aspects of the Kingdom, see *Is the Kingdom of God Realism?*, especially pp. 61–63.

15. *The Christ of the American Road*, pp. 21, 23, 46.

16. *Christ's Alternative to Communism*, p. 270.

17. *Is the Kingdom of God Realism?*, p. 54.

18. *The Christ of the American Road*, p. 45.

19. *Ibid.*, p. 21.

20. *Christ's Alternative to Communism*, p. 222.

21. *Ibid.*, p. 287.

22. *The Choice Before Us*, p. 182.

23. *Is the Kingdom of God Realism?*, pp. 58–59, 63.

24. *The Christ of the American Road*, pp. 201, 205.

25. *Christ's Alternative to Communism*, pp. 221 ff.

26. *Ibid.*, pp. 220 f.

27. *Ibid.*, p. 206.

28. *Ibid.*, p. 224. He makes the same charge on p. 154, using contemptuously the phrase "Christian capitalists."

29. *The Christ of the American Road*, pp. 205–24.

30. The plan for ecclesiastical federation is given in *The Christ of the American Road*, chapter XIV, titled "Federal Union of the Churches and of the Nations."

31. *Christ's Alternative to Communism*, p. 268.

32. *Ibid.*, p. 252.

33. *Ibid.*, pp. 254 f.

34. *The Choice Before Us*, p. 19.

35. *The Christ of the American Road*, pp. 72–73.

36. *Ibid.*, p. 106.

37. *The Choice Before Us*, p. 111.

38. *Christ's Alternative to Communism*, p. 260.

39. *The Choice Before Us*, p. 30.

40. *Christ's Alternative to Communism*, p. 271.

41. *Is the Kingdom of God Realism?*, p. 36.

42. *Ibid.*, p. 263.

43. *Christ's Alternative to Communism*, p. 165. See also *The Christ of the American Road* (pp. 6, 37, 206) where he uses "totalitarian"; but he rejects it as not being an adequate concept on p. 192.

44. *Ibid.*, p. 294.

45. *Christ's Alternative to Communism*, pp. 36 f.

46. *Ibid.*, Chapters I–VI.

47. *Ibid.*, pp. 301 f.

48. *Christ's Alternative to Communism*, pp. 89, 167.

49. *Ibid.*, p. 122.

50. *Ibid.*, pp. 70 f.

51. *Ibid.*, pp. 76 f.

52. *Ibid.*, pp. 72, 78, 90, 138.

53. *Ibid.*, p. 70.

54. *Ibid.*, pp. 166 f.

55. See especially pp. 18, 20, 32, 206, 207, 209.

56. *Ibid.*, p. 138.

57. *Ibid.*, pp. 14, 17, 20, 22. See the whole of Chapter I titled, "Was Jesus a Realist?"

58. *Christ's Alternative to Communism*, pp. 159 f., 294.

59. *Ibid.*, p. 162.

60. *Ibid.*, p. 169.

61. *Ibid.*, p. 299.

62. P. 7.

63. *Christ's Alternative to Communism*, pp. 53, 103, 225, 239.

64. See especially pp. 75, 211, 214–19.

65. *Ibid.*, pp. 240–49.

66. Chapter IX, pp. 221–30.

67. *The Christ of the American Road*, p. 200.

1. *The World's Need of Christ* (1940), Chapter Six.

2. *Christianity and Social Science* (1923), p. 10. This book, as well as several others, was written while Ellwood was Professor of Sociology at the University of Missouri.

3. *Ibid.*, pp. 10–11.

4. *The Reconstruction of Religion* (1922), p. 100.

5. *Ibid.*, p. 98.

6. *Ibid.*, pp. 95, 102–103, 107.

7. *Ibid.*, p. 117.

8. *Man's Social Destiny* (1929), p. 20.

9. *Ibid.*, p. 26.

10. Quoted in *Man's Social Destiny*, p. 25, from *Recent Gains in American Civilization* (1928), edited by K. Page.

11. *The World's Need of Christ*, p. 16.

12. *Ibid.*, p. 41.

13. *Ibid.*, p. 43.

14. *Ibid.*, p. 49.

15. *Ibid.*, pp. 117 f.

16. *Ibid.*, p. 151.

17. *Ibid.*, pp. 152, 153.

18. *Ibid.*, pp. 200 f.

19. *Ibid.*, pp. 91 f.

20. Quoted from *The Choice Before Us* (p. 215) in *The World's Need of Christ*, p. 91.

21. *The Reconstruction of Religion*, p. 211.

22. *Ibid.*, p. 233.

23. *Ibid.*, p. 241.

24. *The World's Need of Christ*, pp. 125, 127.

25. *Ibid.*, p. 127.

26. *The Reconstruction of Religion*, p. 246.

27. *Ibid.*, p. 116 and footnote.

28. *Man's Social Destiny*, pp. 120–24.

29. *Ibid.*, pp. 134 f. Ellwood shows his academic bias, however, by asserting that the chief function of government is to "support and promote education."

30. *The World's Need of Christ*, pp. 158–61.

31. See for example *The Reconstruction of Religion*, especially Chapter VIII, entitled "Religion and Economic Life."

32. *Ibid.*, p. 225.

33. *The Reconstruction of Religion*, p. 1.

34. *Christianity and Social Science*, p. 19. Of course, this last-quoted utterance is based on a certain condition, namely, that "if it were possible to control the learning of all individuals," etc., etc.

35. *Ibid.*, p. 215.

36. *The World's Need of Christ*, pp. 62 f., 64.

37. *Ibid.*, p. 64.

38. *The Reconstruction of Religion*, p. 20.

39. *Ibid.*, p. 18.

40. *Ibid.*, p. 39.

41. Chapter V, titled "Positive Christianity the Religion of Humanity."

42. *Ibid.*, pp. 84 f.

43. *Man's Social Destiny*, p. 217.

44. *Ibid.*, p. 216.

45. *The Reconstruction of Religion*, pp. 1–2, 23, 24, 26, 55, 95; *Christianity and Social Science*, pp. 1, 61, 62, 77, 127, 211; *Man's Social Destiny* (Note that these are but a few random selections from a storehouse).

46. *The World's Need of Christ*, p. 208.

47. He strongly recommends the study of Macintosh's *Social Religion* and Simkhovitch's *Toward the Understanding of Jesus*, suggesting that perhaps an ignorant world would be surprised to discover in the latter work a revelation that "essentially Christ was a peace-seeker and a peace-maker." *The World's Need of Christ*, p. 18n.

48. *Ibid.*, p. 107.

49. *Ibid.*, p. 211.

50. *Ibid.*, pp. 560–61.

51. *Ibid.*, p. 562.

52. *Ibid.*, p. 563.

53. *Ibid.*, p. 564.

54. *The World's Need of Christ*, pp. 198–99.

55. *Ibid.*, pp. 141 f.

56. *Ibid.*, pp. 193–97.

57. *A History of Social Philosophy*, p. 554.

4

1. H. F. Rall, editor, *Religion and Public Affairs* (1937). This honor marked his twenty-fifth year as bishop of the Methodist Episcopal church.

2. *Human Needs and World Christianity* (1929), pp. 79–80.

3. *Public Opinion and Theology* (1920), p. 75.

4. *Ibid.*, p. 82.

5. *Human Needs and World Christianity*, p. 146.

6. *Ibid.*, pp. 176 f.

7. *The Church After the War* (1943), p. 18 f.

8. *Ibid.*, p. 15.

9. *Ibid.*, pp. 12 f. Interestingly enough, McConnell says in regard to the causes of this nineteenth-century militarism and recurrent war, that "this movement was an outcome of the industrial revolution." At this point he emphasizes a

Marxian note by saying that economic problems profoundly "affect human destiny." *Ibid.*, pp. 13–14.

10. *Democratic Christianity* (1919), pp. 48 ff.

11. *Humanism and Christianity* (1928), pp. 55 ff.

12. *The Church After the War*, pp. 78 f., 1943.

13. *Christianity and Coercion* (1933), p. 109.

14. *Ibid.*, p. 121.

15. *Christianity and Coercion*, p. 119.

16. *Ibid.*, p. 120.

17. *Democratic Christianity*, pp. 50 f.

18. *Human Needs and World Christianity*, p. 107. For other attacks on capitalism, its evil fruits and its "unchristian" ethos, see in this volume pp. 44, 56, 61, 65–67, 71–73, 77, 79, 80, 110 f.

19. Strong criticisms are made against competition, the spirit of rivalry, and monopoly control by "financial magnates" in *The Church After the War*, pp. 70 f., 74, 82 f. He also questions the value paid for the so-called service of a "captain of modern competitive industry." *Humanism and Christianity*, p. 72 f.

20. *Human Needs and World Christianity*, p. 77.

21. *Ibid.*, 156.

22. *Christianity and Coercion*, p. 24.

23. *Ibid.*, p. 33.

24. See "Economic Incentives in the New Society," in Kirby Page, editor, *A New Economic Order* (1930), pp. 354 f., where McConnell contends that the stakes are too high in a system of "competition for a chance to win one's daily bread."

25. *Christianity and Coercion*, p. 116.

26. *Democratic Christianity*, p. 51.

27. *Christianity and Coercion*, pp. 24–25.

28. *Democratic Christianity*, p. 21.

29. *Ibid.*, see especially the "Foreword" and pp. 2–3.

30. *The Church After the War*, p. 134.

31. *Ibid.*, pp. 134–35.

32. *Democratic Christianity*, p. 66.

33. *Ibid.*, p. 14.

34. See especially pp. 71, 73, 79, 147.

35. *Ibid.*, p. 75.

36. *Ibid.*, p. 76.

37. *Christianity and Coercion*, pp. 84 f.

38. *The Church After the War*, p. 107.

39. *Ibid.*, p. 108.

40. Article titled "The Church Must Face It!" in the volume *A Basis for the Peace to Come*, p. 22, a collection of the Merrick-McDowell Lectures (1942) at

Ohio Wesleyan University, Delaware, Ohio (Published by the Abingdon-Cokesbury Press).

41. *Democratic Christianity*, p. 40.
42. *Ibid.*, p. 24.
43. *Ibid.*, p. 61.
44. *The Church After the War*, p. 122.
45. *Ibid.*, p. 123.
46. *Ibid.*, p. 135.
47. *Public Opinion and Theology*, p. 185.
48. *Christianity and Coercion*, pp. 99 f.
49. *The Church After the War*, p. 76.

5

1. Among his most recent volumes, 1946, are *The Light Is Still Shining in the Darkness* and *Now Is the Time to Prevent a Third World War*, both copyrighted by himself at La Habra, California. He also has written three books in collaboration with Sherwood Eddy, and edited two others.

2. The very titles of his writings often illustrate the temper or outlook. Cf., for instance, pamphlets like *How Does God Deal with Evildoers?*, *How to Keep America Out of War*, *How Jesus Faced Totalitarianism*, and *Incentives in Modern Life*. The last is subtitled, "Are the Motives of Jesus Practicable in Modern Business and Professional Life?" Significant also are such book titles as *The Sword or the Cross*, or *The Will of God for These Days*, 1945.

3. Published in pamphlet form under the title, *Incentives in Modern Life* (1922).

4. *Ibid.*, p. 25.

5. Copyrighted in 1922 by F. Ernest Johnson and published at the Association Press, New York.

6. *Christianity and Economic Problems*, pp. 113–14.

7. *Ibid.*, p. 2.

8. As a matter of fact Page's central concern during the twenties was the international problem rather than that of domestic economic reconstruction. Volumes such as *War: Its Causes, Consequences, and Cure* (1923), *An American Peace Policy* (1925), *Imperialism and Nationalism* (1925), and *Dollars and World Peace* (1927), are illustrative of his major preoccupation.

9. *Living Creatively*, p. 14.

10. *Ibid.*, pp. 162 f., 164 f., 204 f. In the pamphlet on *Property* (to be examined in more detail presently), after giving his summary of major points against capitalism, he remarks: "Persons who sanction and support this system of economic individualism are as blind as were the men of other days who defended slavery, serfdom, and the divine right of kings" (p. 30).

11. *Ibid.*, p. 326. At the end of the book are found two Appendices, one a

reprint of the 1932 Platform of the Socialist Party of America and the other a reprint of the "Principles and Objectives" of The Fellowship of Socialist Christians, which at the time endorsed the Socialist Party as "most nearly approximating a political expression of Christian ethics for our day."

12. *Capitalism and Its Rivals*, pp. 20, 21.

13. Another excellent account of Page's view of the origin, development and significance of the fascist movement is found in his *Individualism and Socialism*, Chapter VII, titled "The Menace of Fascism."

14. The articles are titled respectively, "Socialism Versus Communism," "A Socialist Program of Deliverance," "Can Socialists and Communists Unite?" "What is Behind the United Front?" and "Revolution: What Kind?" Cf. also his "Comment" on the Appeal to the Socialist Party by a Revolutionary Policy Committee of 47 members (*The World Tomorrow*, April 12, 1934).

15. *Property*, p. 33.

16. *Ibid.*, p. 50.

17. "A Socialist Program of Deliverance," *The World Tomorrow*, May, 1933, p. 323.

18. From the article in *The World Tomorrow*, June 14, 1934, titled "Revolution: What Kind?" p. 303.

19. "Socialism Versus Communism," *The World Tomorrow*, p. 260.

20. Article in *The World Tomorrow*, June, 1932, titled "Is Coercion Ever Justifiable?" p. 174.

21. *Ibid.*, p. 173.

22. *Individualism and Socialism*, pp. 320 f.

23. Article in *The World Tomorrow*, March 1, 1933, titled "Is Coercion Compatible with Religion?" p. 210.

24. In *The World Tomorrow*, January 4, 1934.

25. *Ibid.*, p. 11.

26. Article in *The World Tomorrow*, June, 1932, *op. cit.*, p. 174.

27. "Pacifism and the Class War," *The World Tomorrow*, February 1, 1934.

28. Note that Page is opposed to what he calls "international war" and "civil war on the industrial front." He repeatedly uses phrases like "pacifist revolution" and "non-warlike revolution."

29. In addition to numerous articles, editorials and pamphlets he has released such books as *War: Its Causes, Consequences, and Cure* (1923), *An American Peace Policy* and *Imperialism and Nationalism* (in 1925), *Dollars and World Peace* (1927), *National Defense* (1931), and *Now Is the Time to Prevent a Third World War* (1946). The work published in 1931, *National Defense*, presents an overwhelming array of ugly details about international relations.

30. *The World Tomorrow*, July 26, 1934.

31. *Now Is the Time to Prevent a Third World War*, p. 21.

32. *Ibid.*, p. 25.

33. See Chapter X of *The Will of God for These Days.*

34. See in this connection his work on *Property*, especially pp. 46–50.

35. *Ibid.*, pp. 58 f.

6

1. Chapter I of *Which Way Religion?*, 1931. See also in *The Union Review*, May, 1941, a more recent article, titled "Christianity, An Ethical Religion," in which Ward attacks present religious trends as unfortunate "emphases upon worship, the church, or theology," and pleads for a "cooperation between humanized science and socialized religion" (p. 7).

2. Preface to *The New Social Order*, p. vi.

3. The first was copyrighted in 1918 by the Missionary Movement of the United States and Canada, while the second (copyrighted by the author) was published in 1919, The Woman's Press, New York.

4. *The Opportunity for Religion*, p. 8.

5. *Ibid.*, p. 10.

6. In fact his championship of labor went back into the pre-war era. Cf. for instance titles by him such as "The Labor Movement," in his *Social Ministry* (1910), and *Poverty and Wealth* (1915).

7. Examples of his treatment of the subject are found in articles like "Is the Profit Motive An Economic Necessity?" and "Is Profit Christian?" published respectively in *The Christian Century* for June 28, and December 27, 1923. But the extent to which his mind was preoccupied with the issue of economic incentives and moral idealism can be seen most clearly in *Our Economic Morality*, 1929, and *In Place of Profit*, 1933, which volumes will be examined presently in more detail.

8. From the Preface (p. vii) and p. 3.

9. Article titled "How Can Civilization Be Saved?" in *The Christian Century*, September 11, 1924, pp. 1176 f. But his attraction was not unqualified. He says in the same context that "reform is inadequate and revolution is too drastic"; we must replace gradually like a railroad station being "rebuilt while traffic still runs in and out of it." For a still more vigorous criticism of Soviet policy see also his articles "Will Religion Survive in Russia?" (*The Christian Century*, Feb. 12, 1925) and "Civil Liberties in Russia" (*The Nation*, March 4, 1925).

10. The first, written after a period of study in Russia in 1931–32, was published by Charles Scribner's Sons, New York, the second by the International Publishers, Inc., New York.

11. From the Preface to *In Place of Profit*, p. viii.

12. *The Soviet Spirit*, pp. 9, 11 (paper edition).

13. *In Place of Profit*, p. 212.

14. *Ibid.*, p. 219.

15. *The Soviet Spirit*, p. 15.

16. *In Place of Profit*, p. 233.

17. *The Soviet Spirit*, p. 62.

18. *Ibid.*, p. 158. It is interesting, however, that in defense of the liberties of the masses and the evolving democratic nature of the Soviet Government Ward relies mainly upon quotations from writings and speeches of authorities. See especially in this connection *In Place of Profit*, pp. 219–264. Cf. also an article titled "Official Protestantism and Soviet Aims" (in *The Protestant*, May 1944) in which he quotes abundantly from Stalin's speeches of Nov. 6, 1941, 1942 and 1943 to prove the benevolent purposes of Russia's military and diplomatic policies.

19. The *Christian Century*, March 31, 1943, p. 390.

20. In *Democracy and Social Change*, see Chapter XIII on "The Role of Religion" and Chapters VII and XIV for his defense of a democratic method and of civil liberties.

21. "It Is Time to Fight," *The Protestant*, August–September, 1943, pp. 171–72.

22. *Ibid.*, p. 180.

23. Titled, "The Red Scare" and "The Class Line-Up."

7

1. One of the few instances of direct criticism is found in *An Interpretation of Christian Ethics* (1935), pp. 172–81, where he refers to the Federal Council's endorsement of the NRA program, as well as to writers like Shailer Mathews, G. B. Smith, Francis J. McConnell and E. Stanley Jones.

2. A British writer, D. R. Davies, has recently produced a tiny volume titled *Reinhold Niebuhr: Prophet from America* (undated, but probably 1945) in which he contended that here is an American who is the most significant "Christian revolutionary" in the Western World. The Swedish theologian, George Hammar, refers to his thinking as "a central and unique position within contemporary American theology" (*Christian Realism in Contemporary American Theology*, 1940, p. 249).

3. These phrases have been used as chapter headings in the aforementioned volume, *Reinhold Niebuhr: Prophet from America*, by Davies. One of the misleading aspects of this excellent, illuminating study is the fact that the "movement to the right" is treated in such a manner as to leave room for the assumption that Niebuhr has merely restored historic Christian orthodoxy.

4. Article titled "The Contribution of Reinhold Niebuhr" in *Religion in Life*, spring number, 1937, p. 270. In this context Bennett lists nine thought-systems or intellectual viewpoints which deeply influence Niebuhr, and yet viewpoints "which at some points he rejects."

5. *Christianity and Power Politics*, p. 28.

6. The first two were published in 1932, the third in 1934. The earliest volume was the publication of The Forbes Lectures of the New York School of Social Work, lectures actually delivered in 1930.

7. *The Contribution of Religion to Social Work*, p. 77.

8. *Ibid.*, pp. 80, 82.

9. *Ibid.*, pp. 83, 84, 87, 88, 94.

10. Norman Thomas wrote a lengthy review in *The World Tomorrow*, December 14, 1932. While praising the work highly at many points, he nevertheless charged that Niebuhr gave the "impression of defeatism." For Niebuhr's reply to the critics see his article, "Optimism and Utopianism," in *The World Tomorrow*, Feb. 22, 1933.

11. *Christian Realism in Contemporary American Theology*, p. 181.

12. Title of Chapter VI.

13. Niebuhr acknowledges that this presentation is only a "tentative adjustment between Christian and Socialist thought." "Many members of the organization," he submits, "would not agree with it." See also by him articles in *The World Tomorrow* (1933) for March 1, July, August 31 and December 21 titled respectively "After Capitalism—What?", "A Reorientation of Radicalism," "A New Strategy for Socialists" and "Making Radicalism Effective."

14. *An Interpretation of Christian Ethics*, p. 5.

15. *The Nature and Destiny of Man*, II, 156.

16. *The Children of Light and the Children of Darkness*, p. 151.

17. *Ibid.*, pp. 132–33.

18. Niebuhr criticizes Paul for uncritical submission to government as a power ordained by God. He charges the Apostle with having been "very 'undialectical.' " *Ibid.*, p. 270.

8

1. Published by Willett-Clark & Co., copyright 1935. The first-mentioned author is H. Richard Niebuhr of the Yale Divinity School, Yale University, brother of Reinhold Niebuhr.

2. See especially Tillich's *The Religious Situation* (1932), *The Interpretation of History* (1936), and his article in *The Christian Answer* (1945), edited by Van Dusen.

3. Kean is a member of the Executive Committee of the Fellowship of Socialist Christians and the rector of Grace Episcopal Church in Kirkwood, Mo. Bennett is Professor of Christian Theology and Ethics at the Union Theological Seminary and an active member of the Fellowship of Socialist Christians.

4. *The Christian Answer*, pp. 27 f.

5. *The Nature and Destiny of Man*, I, 27–29.

6. *Christianity and the Cultural Crisis*, pp. 3–13.

7. *Op. cit.*, pp. 31, 33.

8. *Op. cit.*, p. 10.

9. *The Nature and Destiny of Man*, II, 154–55.

10. *Op. cit.*, p. 44.

11. *The Christian Answer*, p. 27.

12. *The Nature and Destiny of Man*, II, 65 f.

13. *Ibid.*, I, 13.

14. See especially his *What Is Christianity?* (1940). The author has discussed Morrison's theory of the church in some detail in a previous work, *Rethinking Our Christianity* (1942), pp. 170–89.

15. For an excellent account of the fresh significance of the church now being discovered by these "realistic" Christians see Bennett, *Christian Ethics and Social Policy*, Chap. V entitled, "The Ethical Role of the Church in Society."

16. *We Are Not Divided*, p. 106.

17. *Op. cit.*, pp. 16, 18.

18. *We Are Not Divided*, p. 105.

19. The author has given a brief account of the doctrinal basis of liberal Christianity in his book, *Rethinking Our Christianity*, pp. 124–47.

Selected Bibliography

Chapter 1

Bennett, John Coleman, Social Salvation (New York: Scribners, 1935).
Christianity and Our World (New York: Association Press, 1936).
—— "The Social Interpretation of Christianity," in The Church Through Half a Century, edited by Cavert and Van Dusen (New York: Scribners, 1936).
—— Christian Ethics and Social Policy (New York: Scribners, 1946).
Bodein, Vernon Parker, The Social Gospel of Walter Rauschenbusch and Its Relation to Religious Education (New Haven: Yale University, 1936).
Dombrowski, James, The Early Days of Christian Socialism in America (New York: Columbia University, 1936).
Everett, John Rutherford, Religion in Economics; a Study of John Bates Clark, Richard T. Ely, Simon N. Patten (New York: King's Crown, 1947).
Fosdick, Harry Emerson, Christianity and Progress (New York: Revell, 1922).
—— Adventurous Religion and Other Essays (New York: Harpers, 1926).
Hammar, George, Christian Realism in Contemporary American Theology (Uppsala, Sweden, 1940).
Hopkins, Charles Howard, The Rise of the Social Gospel in American Protestantism (New Haven: Yale University, 1940).
Hutchison, John Alexander, We Are Not Divided (New York: Round Table, 1941) History of the Federal Council of Churches.
Johnson, Frederick Ernest, ed., The Social Work of the Churches (New York: published by The Federal Council, 1930).
—— ed., Christianity and Economic Problems (New York: Association Press, 1922).
—— Economics and the Good Life (New York: Association Press, 1922). Written with group of consultants.
—— Church and Society (New York: Abingdon, 1935).
—— The Social Gospel Re-Examined (New York: Harper, 1940).
McGiffert, Jr., Arthur Cushman, "Walter Rauschenbusch: Twenty Years After," in Christendom, Vol. III (1938).
McNeill, John Thomas, Christian Hope for World Society (Chicago: Willett-Clark, 1937).

Mathews, Shailer, "The Social Gospel," Chapter IX in his New Faith for Old (New York: Macmillan, 1936).

Morrison, Charles Clayton, The Social Gospel and the Christian Cultus (New York: Harpers, 1933).

———— (Editorial) "Orthodoxy, Too, Has Its Social Gospel," in *The Christian Century* (March 1, 1944).

———— (Editorial) "Is There a Social Gospel?" in *The Christian Century* (March 15, 1944).

Nixon, Justin Wroe, "Peace and the Social Gospel," in *Christianity and Crisis* (October 6, 1941).

Rauschenbusch, Walter, Christianity and the Social Crisis (New York: Macmillan, 1907).

———— Christianizing the Social Order (New York: Macmillan, 1912, 1926).

———— A Theology for the Social Gospel (New York: Macmillan, 1917).

Schroeder, John Charles, "A Deeper Social Gospel," in *The Christian Century* (July 26, 1939).

Visser't Hooft, Willem Adolph, The Background of the Social Gospel in America (New York: Oxford, 1928).

Williams, Melvin J., "Representative Sociological Contributions to Religion and Ethics" in Barnes and Becker, (ed.), Contemporary Social Theory (New York: D. Appleton–Century, 1940).

Chapter 2

Jones, Eli Stanley, The Christ of the Indian Road (New York: Abingdon, 1925).

———— Along the Indian Road, a sequel (New York: Abingdon, 1939).

———— Christ's Alternative to Communism (New York: Abingdon, 1935).

———— The Choice before Us (New York: Abingdon, 1937).

———— Is the Kingdom of God Realism? (Abingdon-Cokesbury, 1941).

———— Abundant Living (Abingdon-Cokesbury, 1942).

———— The Christ of the American Road (Abingdon-Cokesbury, 1944).

Articles by Jones in *The Christian Century:*

"Christians of America, Unite!" (October 2, 1935).

"An Open Letter to the People of Japan" (September 15, 1937).

"An Open Letter to the Christian People of America and Great Britain" (November 10, 1937).

"The University Christian Mission" (January 4, 1939).

"Apply the Gandhi Method to Japan!" (February 8, 1939).

"Where Madras Missed the Way" (March 15, 1939).
"The Christ of the Kingdom" (May 3, 1939).
"What I Missed at Madras" (May 31, 1939).
"How Shall We Pray in Time of War?" (February 7, 1940).
"America United—On What Level?" (September 17, 1941).
"What Should We Do Now?" (December 31, 1941).
"Barbed-Wire Christians" (November 24, 1943).

Chapter 3

Ellwood, Charles Abram, Sociology and Modern Social Problems (New York: American Book Co., 1919 and 1924); Re-issued in 1935 as Social Problems and Sociology.
——— The Reconstruction of Religion (New York: Macmillan, 1922).
——— Christianity and Social Science (New York: Macmillan, 1923).
——— The Psychology of Human Society, subtitled An Introduction to Sociological Theory (New York: D. Appleton, 1925).
——— Cultural Evolution: A Study of Social Origins and Development (New York: The Century Co., 1927).
——— The Social Problem; A Reconstructive Analysis (Rev. Ed., New York: Macmillan, 1929).
——— Man's Social Destiny (Nashville: Cokesbury, 1929).
——— Emasculated Sociologies (New York: The Social Science Publishing Co., 1933).
——— A History of Social Philosophy (New York: Prentice-Hall, 1938).
——— The World's Need of Christ (New York: Abingdon-Cokesbury, 1940).
Articles by Ellwood in Fellowship, organ of the Fellowship of Reconciliation:
"Christian Democracy and Violence" (April, 1938).
"The Fight Has Just Begun" (February, 1943).
"War and the Totalitarian State" (April, 1943).
"Pacifism and Social Evolution" (July, 1943).
Other articles by Ellwood:
"Religion and Social Control," in The Scientific Monthly (October, 1918).
"Recent Developments in Sociology," in the volume, Recent Developments in the Social Sciences (New York: Lippincott, 1927).
Cf. also Jensen, Howard E., "Development of the Social Thought of Charles Abram Ellwood," in Sociology and Social Research (May–June, 1947).

Chapter 4

McConnell, Francis John, Democratic Christianity (New York: Macmillan, 1919).
—— Public Opinion and Theology (New York: Abingdon, 1920).
—— Humanism and Christianity (New York: Macmillan, 1928).
—— Human Needs and World Christianity (New York: Friendship Press, 1929).
—— Christianity and Coercion (Nashville: Cokesbury, 1933).
—— Christian Materialism (New York: Friendship Press, 1936).
—— The Church after the War (New York: Board of Missions and Church Extension of the Methodist Church, 1943).
Articles by McConnell:
"Economic Incentives in the New Society," in Page, ed., A New Economic Order (New York: Harcourt, Brace, 1930).
"What is Defense?" in Fellowship, organ of the Fellowship of Reconciliation (March, 1937).
"From Lausanne to Munich," in The Christian Century (April 19, 1939).
"The Church Must Face It," in the volume A Basis for the Peace to Come (New York: Abingdon-Cokesbury, 1942).
"Christian Tests of Society," in the Social Questions Bulletin of the Methodist Federation for Social Service (January, 1943).
"Religion and Democracy," in Religion and World Order, F. Ernest Johnson, ed. (New York: Harpers, 1944).
Works revealing McConnell's Personalistic theology:
McConnell, Francis John, Personal Christianity: Instruments and Ends in the Kingdom of God (New York: Revell, 1914).
—— Religious Certainty (New York: Eaton & Mains; Cincinnati: Jennings & Graham, 1910).
—— The Diviner Immanence (New York: Eaton & Mains; Cincinnati: Jennings & Graham, 1910).
—— Is God Limited? (New York: Abingdon, 1924).
—— Aids to Christian Belief (New York: Abingdon, 1932).
—— "Fact and Faith" in the volume Religious Life, E. Sapir and others (New York: D. Van Nostrand, 1929).
Cf. also Rall, Harris F., ed., Religion and Public Affairs (New York: Macmillan, 1937). Essays in honor of Bishop McConnell.

Chapter 5

Page, Kirby, Christianity and Economic Problems (New York: Association Press, 1922). A discussion group text book.
———— An American Peace Policy (Garden City: Doran, 1925).
———— Imperialism and Nationalism (Garden City: Doran, 1925).
———— Dollars and World Peace (Garden City: Doran, 1925).
———— Jesus or Christianity (Garden City: Doubleday, Doran, 1929).
———— ed., A New Economic Order (New York: Harcourt, Brace, 1930).
———— National Defense (New York: Farrar and Rinehart, 1933).
———— Living Creatively (New York: Farrar and Rinehart, 1932).
———— Individualism and Socialism (New York: Farrar and Rinehart, 1933).
———— Religious Resources for Personal Living and Social Action (New York: Farrar and Rinehart, 1939).
———— The Will of God for These Days (copyrighted by the author at La Habra, California, 1945).
———— The Light Is Still Shining in the Darkness (copyrighted by the author at La Habra, California, 1946).
———— Now Is the Time to Prevent a Third World War (copyrighted by the author at La Habra, California, 1946).
Pamphlets by Kirby Page:
Collective Bargaining (Garden City: Doran, 1921).
Incentives in Modern Life (William Penn Lecture) (Garden City: Doran, 1922).
The Abolition of War (with Eddy) (Garden City: Doran, 1924).
Dollars and World Peace (with Eddy) (Garden City: Doran, 1927).
What Shall We Do about War? (with Eddy) (copyrighted by Eddy and Page, New York, undated, but possibly 1935 or 1936).
Capitalism and Its Rivals (copyrighted by Eddy and Page, probably about 1935).
Property (copyrighted by Eddy and Page, probably about 1935).
If War Is Sin (under auspices of Fellowship of Reconciliation, 1935).
Articles by Kirby Page in *The World Tomorrow:*
"Is Coercion Ever Justifiable?" (June, 1932).
"Socialism versus Communism" (October 14, 1932).
"Is Coercion Compatible with Religion?" (March 1, 1933).
"A Socialist Program of Deliverance" (April 5, 1933).
"Can Socialists and Communists Unite?" (October 26, 1933).
"The Future of the Fellowship" (January 4, 1934).
"Pacifism and Class War" (February 1, 1934).

"Comment" on an "Appeal to the Socialist Party" (by a Revolutionary Policy Committee). April 12, 1934.
"Revolution: What Kind?" (June 14, 1934).
"If War Is to Be Abolished" (July 26, 1934).
Other Articles by Kirby Page:
"The Christian View of Society," in Dynamic Faith, ed. by Porter (New York: Association Press, 1927).
"International Economic Co-operation," Chapter XII in the volume, A New Economic Order, ed. by Page (New York: Harcourt, Brace, 1930).
"The Cross and Social Change," in *Fellowship* (November, 1936).
"Pacifism Can Stop Aggression," in the pamphlet Pacifism and Aggression (New York, 1938).

Chapter 6

Ward, Harry Frederick, The Social Creed of the Churches (copyright by the editor-author, 1912).
—— Poverty and Wealth, From the viewpoint of the kingdom of God (New York: Methodist Book Concern, 1915).
—— The Labor Movement from the Standpoint of Religious Values (copyrighted by the Missionary Movement of the United States and Canada, 1918).
—— The Opportunity for Religion (New York: The Woman's Press, 1919).
—— The New Social Order (New York: Macmillan, 1919).
—— Our Economic Morality and the Ethic of Jesus (New York: Macmillan, 1929).
—— Which Way Religion? (New York: Macmillan, 1931).
—— In Place of Profit (New York: Scribners, 1933).
—— Democracy and Social Change (New York: Modern Age Books, Inc., 1940).
—— The Soviet Spirit (New York: International Publishers, 1944).
Articles by Ward in *The Christian Century*:
"The Competitive System and the Mind of Jesus" (June 9, 1921).
"Is the Profit Motive an Economic Necessity?" (June 28, 1923).
"How Can Civilization Be Saved?" (September 28, 1928).
"Will Religion Survive in Russia?" (February 12, 1925).
"Gandhi and the Future of India" (June 4, 1925).
"China Learns from the West" (July 30, 1925).
"China's Industrial Battlefront" (March 18, 1926).
"China's Anti-Christian Movement" (April 15, 1926).

"China's Anti-Christian Temper" (May 13, 1926).
"Religion and Justice" (February 7, 1929).
"Religion and Political Corruption" (June 12, 1929).
"Religion Confronts a New World" (February 3, 1932).
"Is Profit Christian?" (December 27, 1933).
"Judgment Day for the Pacifists" (December 18, 1935).
"Christians and Communists" (December 25, 1935).
"Liberalism at the Crisis" (March 25, 1936).
"The Morals of Reaction" (November 16, 1938).
"The Future of the Profit Motive" (March 31, 1943).
"The Moral Equivalent of War" (July 14, 1943).
"Fascist Trends in the Churches" (April 19, 1944).
"Vatican Fascism" (June 7, 1944).
Articles and pamphlets by Ward under auspices of the American League
Against War and Fascism and the American League for Peace and De-
mocracy:
"Ethiopia" in *Fight,* organ of American League Against War and
Fascism (February, 1936).
The Neutrality Issue (pamphlet), American League for Peace and
Democracy (April, 1938).
Concerted Action for Peace (pamphlet), American League for Peace
and Democracy (April, 1938).
"The Fascist International" (March, 1937).
"Development of Fascism in the United States" (undated).
Other Articles by Ward:
"The Bible and the Proletarian Movement," in the *Journal of Religion*
(May, 1921).
"American Christianity and Social Idealism," extract from *American
Review Magazine* (July–August, 1923).
"Civil Liberties in Russia," in *The Nation* (March 4, 1925).
"Lenin and Gandhi," in *The World Tomorrow* (April, 1925).
"Will Russia Return to Capitalism?" in *The Nation* (July 8, 1925).
"The Challenge of Unemployment Relief in Religious Education,"
in *The China Outlook* (March 1, 1931).
"Pioneers Among the Soviets," in *The Nation* (June 22, 1932).
"The International Situation and America's Relation to It," in *Radical
Religion* (Summer, 1939).
"The Dies Committee and Civil Liberties," in *The Union Review*
(December, 1939).
"Debs, Bourne, and Reed," in *New Masses* (March 4, 1941).
"The Crime of Thinking," in *New Masses* (April 22, 1941).
"Christianity, an Ethical Religion," in *The Union Review* (May, 1941).
"The Anti-Soviet Front and Its Objectives" in *The Protestant* (April–
May, 1942).

"Protestants and the Anti-Soviet Front," in *The Protestant* (December–January, 1942).

"It Is Time to Fight," in *The Protestant* (1943).

"Reader's Digest Capitalism," in *The Protestant* (Vol. IV, No. 10, 1943).

"Official Protestantism and Soviet Aims," in *The Protestant* (May, 1944).

See Ward's address to Methodists, "Social Unrest in the United States," together with a letter on the Russian situation issued by the Methodist Federation for Social Service, March, 1919.

Cf. also an article by Graham Taylor on "The 'Bolshevism' of Professor Ward" in the *Survey*, March 29, 1919.

Chapter 7

Niebuhr, Reinhold, Does Civilization Need Religion? (New York: Macmillan, 1927).

—— Leaves from the Notebook of a Tamed Cynic (Chicago: Willet Clark and Colby, 1929).

—— The Contribution of Religion to Social Work (New York: Columbia University Press, 1930). The Forbes Lectures of the New York School of Social Work.

—— Moral Man and Immoral Society (New York: Scribners, 1933).

—— Reflections on the End of an Era (New York: Scribners, 1934).

—— An Interpretation of Christian Ethics (New York: Harpers, 1935).

—— Beyond Tragedy (New York: Scribners, 1938).

—— Christianity and Power Politics (New York: Scribners, 1940). A collection of essays and articles.

—— The Nature and Destiny of Man, 2 vols. (New York: Scribners, 1941–43) Gifford Lectures for 1939.

—— The Children of Light and the Children of Darkness (New York: Scribners, 1944).

—— Discerning the Signs of the Times (New York: Scribners, 1946). A book of sermons.

Articles by Niebuhr in *The World Tomorrow:*

"Why We Need a New Economic Order" (1928).

"Is Peace or Justice the Goal?" (September 21, 1932).

"Idealists and the Social Struggle" (October 26, 1932).

"After Capitalism—What?" (March 1, 1933).

"A Reorientation of Radicalism" (July, 1933).

"A New Strategy for Socialists" (August 31, 1933).

"Making Radicalism Effective" (December 21, 1933).
"Shall We Seek World Peace or the Peace of America?" (March 15, 1934).
"Comment" on a revolutionary "Appeal to the Socialist Party" (April 12, 1934).
"The Fellowship of Socialist Christians" (June 14, 1934).
"The Problem of Communist Religion" (July 26, 1934).
Articles by Niebuhr in *Christianity and Society* (formerly *Radical Religion*):
"The Idea of Progress and Socialism," in *Radical Religion* (Spring, 1936).
"The Creed of Modern Christian Socialists," in *Radical Religion* (1938).
"The Perils of Our Foreign Policy" (Spring, 1943).
Articles by Niebuhr in *Christianity and Crisis*:
"The Christian Faith and the World Crisis" (February 10, 1941).
"Pacifism and America First" (June 16, 1941).
"Plans for World Reorganization" (October 19, 1942).
"The Christian and the War" (November 16, 1942). Criticism of *The Christian Century*'s position on the war.
"American Power and World Responsibility" (April 5, 1943).
"Anglo-Saxon Destiny and Responsibility" (October 4, 1943).
"We Are in Peril" (October 18, 1943).
"The German Problem" (January 10, 1944).
"The Christian Perspective on the World Crisis" (May 1, 1944).
See also Niebuhr's brief observations on Britain in the war crisis in the issues of June 28, July 12, and July 26, 1943.
Other articles by Niebuhr:
"The Confession of a Tired Radical," in *The Christian Century* (August 20, 1928).
"Christianity and Redemption," in Whither Christianity, ed. by Hough (New York: Harpers, 1929).
"Political Action and Social Change," in A New Economic Order, ed. by Page (New York: Harcourt, Brace, 1930).
"Why I Leave the F.O.R.," in *The Christian Century* (January 3, 1934).
"Christian Politics and Communist Religion," in Christianity and the Social Revolution, ed. by John Lewis (New York: Scribners, 1936).
"Christian Faith and the Common Life," in the Oxford Conference Book of the same title (Chicago: Willett, Clark, 1938).
"Ten Years That Shook My World," in *The Christian Century* (April 26, 1939).
"The Contribution of Paul Tillich," in *Religion in Life* (Autumn, 1937).

[175]

"Palestine: British-American Dilemma," in *The Nation* (August 31, 1946).
"Europe, Russia and the United States," in *The Nation* (September 14, 1946).
"Our Relations with Russia," in Christianity Takes a Stand, ed. by William Scarlett (New York: Penguin Books, Inc., 1946).
See also article by A. T. Mollegen in *Christianity and Society* (Spring, 1943), entitled "The Common Convictions of the Fellowship of Socialist Christians" (repeated in 1944).
For interpretations and criticisms of Niebuhr see the following:
MacGregor, G. H. C., "The Relevance of an Impossible Ethical Ideal," in *The Christian Pacifist* (London) and reprinted in *Fellowship* (part two) for June, 1941.
Demant, V. A., "Niebuhr, the Dialectical Moralist," in *Theology* (January, 1944).
Bennett, John C., "The Contribution of Reinhold Niebuhr," in *Religion in Life* (Spring, 1937).
Hammar, George, Christian Realism in Contemporary American Theology (Uppsala, Sweden, 1940). Cf. especially pp. 60–63 and 167–253.
Davies, D. R., Reinhold Niebuhr: Prophet From America (London: James Clarke and Co., Ltd., 1945).

Chapter 8

Aubrey, Edwin Ewart, Present Theological Tendencies (New York: Harpers, 1936).
Baillie, John, What Is Christian Civilization? (New York: Scribners, 1945).
Bennett, John Coleman, "After Liberalism—What?" in *The Christian Century* (November 8, 1933).
——— "New Emphases in Christian Social Teaching," in The Church Faces the World, ed. by Cavert (1939).
——— "Limitations of the Church-Inherent and Accidental," in *Christendom* (1946).
——— "The Causes of Social Evil," in the Oxford Conference Book, Vol. IV, Christian Faith and the Common Life (Chicago: Willett-Clark, 1938).
——— Christian Realism (New York: Scribners, 1941).
——— "The Christian Ethic and Political Responsiblity," in *Christianity and Crisis* (February 24, 1941).

———— "The Christian Conception of Man," in Liberal Theology, ed. by Roberts and Van Dusen (New York: Scribners, 1942).

———— "Enduring Bases of Social Action," in *Social Action* (June 15, 1943).

———— "The Christian Basis for Enduring Peace," a reprint of Chapter XLVIII of the Conference on Science, Philosophy, and Religion in Their Relation to the Democratic Way of Life (New York, 1943).

———— "A Manifesto of Shared Convictions," in *Christendom,* 1944, (a review of The Vitality of the Christian Tradition, ed. by G. F. Thomas [1944]).

———— "Realistic Theology and Social Action," in *Christianity and Society* (Summer, 1945).

———— "The Meaning of Redemption in Personal and Social Life Today," pamphlet reprint from *The Journal of Religious Thought* (Howard University, Autumn–Winter, 1946).

———— Christian Ethics and Social Policy (New York: Scribners, 1946).

Eliot, Thomas Stearns, The Idea of a Christian Society (New York: Harcourt, Brace, 1940).

Easton, William Burnet, Jr., The Faith of a Protestant (New York: Macmillan, 1946).

Hammar, George, Christian Realism in Contemporary American Theology (Uppsala, Sweden, 1940).

Homrighausen, Elmer George. Christianity in America (New York: Abingdon, 1936).

———— Let the Church Be the Church (New York: Abingdon, 1940).

———— Choose Ye This Day (Philadelphia: Westminster Press, 1943).

Horton, Walter Marshall, Realistic Theology (New York: Harpers, 1934).

———— Theology in Transition (New York: Harpers, 1934). Abbreviated reprint of his A Psychological Approach to Theology and Realistic Theology.

———— "Between Liberalism and the New Orthodoxy," in *The Christian Century* (May 17, 1939).

Hughley, Judge Neal, Rethinking Our Christianity (Philadelphia: Dorrance, 1942).

Kean, Charles Duell, "A Christian Insight into Post-war Economics" *Christianity and Society* (Summer, 1944).

———— Christianity and the Cultural Crisis (New York: Association Press, 1945).

———— The Meaning of Existence (New York: Harpers, 1947).

Lewis, Edwin, A Christian Manifesto (1934).

———— The Faith We Declare (1939).

Lewis, Edwin, The Practice of the Christian Life (Philadelphia: Westminster Press, 1942).

Morrison, Charles Clayton, What Is Christianity? (Chicago: Willett-Clark, 1940).

Mackay, John Alexander, A Preface to Christian Theology (New York: Macmillan, 1941).

Niebuhr, Helmut Richard, "Religious Realism in the Twentieth Century," in Religious Realism, ed. by MacIntosh (New York: Macmillan, 1931).

———— The Kingdom of God in America (1937).

———— with Pauck, Miller, The Church Against the World (Chicago: Willett-Clark, 1935).

Niebuhr, Reinhold (See bibliography under Chapter VII).

Smith, H. Shelton, Faith and Nurture (New York: Scribners, 1941).

Trueblood, Eldon, The Predicament of Modern Man (New York: Harpers, 1944).

Tillich, Paul J., The Religious Situation (New York: Henry Holt, 1932). Translated by H. Richard Niebuhr.

———— "The Totalitarian State and the Claims of the Church," in Social Research (November, 1934).

———— "Natural and Revealed Religion," in Christendom (Autumn, 1935).

———— "Marx and the Prophetic Tradition," in Radical Religion (Autumn, 1935).

———— "What Is Wrong with the 'Dialectic' Theology?" in the Journal of Religion (April, 1935).

———— The Interpretation of History (New York: Scribners, 1936).

———— "The Church and Communism," in Religion in Life (Summer, 1937).

———— "Protestantism in the Present World Situation," in the American Journal of Sociology (September, 1937).

———— "The Gospel and the State," in The Crozer Quarterly (October, 1938).

———— "The Kingdom of God and History," in the Oxford Conference Series under same title (Chicago: Willett-Clark, 1938).

———— "The Conception of Man in Existential Philosophy," in the Journal of Religion (July, 1939).

———— "Our Disintegrating World," in the Anglican Theological Review (April, 1941).

———— "The Permanent Significance of the Catholic Church for Protestantism," in the Protestant Digest (February–March, 1941).

———— "Spiritual Problems of Post-War Reconstruction," in Christianity and Crisis (August 10, 1942).

[178]

———— "Marxism and Christian Socialism," in *Christianity and Society* (Spring, 1942).

———— "Man and Society in Religious Socialism," in *Christianity and Society* (Fall, 1943).

———— "Estrangement and Reconciliation in Modern Thought," in *The Review of Religion* (New York, 1944).

———— "Trends in Religious Thought That Affect Social Outlooks," in Religion and the World Order, ed. by F. E. Johnson (New York: Harpers, 1944).

———— "The God of History," in *Christianity and Crisis* (May 1, 1944).

———— "The World Situation," in The Christian Answer, ed. by Van Dusen (New York: Scribners, 1945).

Cf. on Tillich, also Niebuhr's article, "The Contribution of Paul Tillich," in *Religion in Life* (Autumn number, 1937).

Van Dusen, Henry Pitney "The Sickness of Liberal Religion," in *The World Tomorrow* (1931).

———— ed. The Christian Answer (New York: Scribners, 1945).

———— "What Is the Church?" in the *Journal of Religion* (1937).

———— For the Healing of the Nations (New York: Scribners, 1940).

———— What Is the Church Doing? (New York: Scribners, 1945).

Wright, Robert R., "A Next Step in Theology," in *Christianity and Society* (Spring, 1947).

Index

Natural man, 150; Ellwood on, 50
Nazism, 18, 23; Niebuhr against, 110
Negroes, 69
Neo-orothdoxy, 131, 132 n, 133; and Reinhold Niebuhr, 106, 122, 127-128; attack on secularism, 154; challenges the social gospel, 20; first echoes of, 16; meaning of, 132; supernaturalism of, 149
Neo-Protestantism, 16-17; see also Neo-orthodoxy
Niebuhr, H. Richard, 133, 165
New Deal, Page on, 77; Niebuhr on, 118-119; Ward on, 103

Orthodox Christianity, see Christian orthodoxy

Pacifism, and Niebuhr, 108, 109, 110, 125 n; as social gospel idealism, 20; Ellwood on, 43; McConnell on, 62; of Kirby Page, 74, 83-84, 87-88
Pessimism, Ellwood's attack on, 49; in *Moral Man and Immoral Society*, 115-116; in *Reflections on the End of an Era*, 118; Niebuhr's type of, 130
Profit motive, Page on, 161; Ward on, 94, 95, 100, 101-102, 163
Puritan tradition, 3

Rauschenbusch, Walter, 3, 6, 8, 9, 12, 13, 19, 26, 89, 143-144, 155; date of death, 3
Roman Catholicism, 4
Russian revolution, 90, 149; see also Soviet Russia

Secularism, 2, 18; Neo-orthodoxy's attack on, 136, 150; Niebuhr a critic of, 107-108
Single-tax movement, 8, 10
Social gospel, ambiguity of, 1; and

orthodox Christianity, 3; and the dialectical theologians, 19; as social gospel idealism, 4; Ellwood an example of, 140, 145; Jones an example of, 145; McConnell an example of, 145; meaning of, 155; Neo-orthodoxy's attack on, 145-148; Niebuhr's criticism of, 164; official endorsement of, 7; Page an example of, 145; revolt against, 17-19; theological assumptions of, 2; theological position of, 146; utopianism in, 2; variety of patterns of, 5, 7; view of Jesus, 144, 146; view of the church, 144; Ward an example of, 140, 145; Ward on, 98; see also Social gospel outlook
Social gospel idealism, 7; in early twentieth century, 12, 14-15; nineteenth-century forms of, 9-15; of Edward Bellamy, 11; of Henry George, 11; see also Social gospel; Social gospel outlook
Social gospel mentality, Niebuhr's break with, 114
Social gospel movement, Niebuhr's relation to, 105-106
Social gospel outlook, Coe an example of, 26 n; Ellwood an example of, 39, 42, 52; McConnell an example of, 66, 69-70; Page an example of, 88; see also Social gospel; Social gospel tradition
Social gospel tradition, Ellwood, Page, Jones, and Ward as examples of, 24, 26, 45, 49, 73-74, 90, 92, 104; see also Social gospel; Social gospel idealism
Socialism, McConnell on, 57, 58, 59-60, 61, 62, 63; Page on, 85
Social justice, Niebuhr's view of, 126
Social planning, 78, 79; Ward on, 98 n.
Social progress, and Neo-orthodoxy,